Swimming
everyone

• • • • • • • • • • •

Second Edition

Yvonne Messner

 Hunter Textbooks Inc.

⊞ Hunter Textbooks Inc.

823 Reynolda Road
Winston-Salem, North Carolina 27104

PREFACE

Swimming is considered to be the best exercise for everyone, from thin to obese, from tot to elderly, from able-bodied to disabled. The history of swimming dates back to prehistoric times when swimming was necessary for survival and sustenance. Today, its popularity continues for recreational and competitive pursuits.

The primary objectives of this book are to provide the novice swimmer with a simplified analysis of the basic strokes and diving techniques, information on the equipment and supplies used in the water, health and safety measures, and information on the abundance of water sports available today for recreational enjoyment. To be able to swim is to be able to fill one's life with a whole new world of leisure opportunities.

The material in this text is organized in four sections with each dealing with an important area of swimming knowledge. The appendices are designed to supplement the student's assessment of his skills and knowledge, and to offer information for using swimming as a lifetime fitness activity.

ACKNOWLEDGEMENTS

The authors would like to express deep appreciation to several individuals who assisted in the preparation of this book. Sincere thanks to Dr. David Costill, Director of the Ball State University Human Performance Lab, for his willingness to take the needed photographs; to Mr. John Wingfield, Ball State University Director of Aquatics, for picture taking arrangements; to Liz Whitney, Tim Siefker, and Tom Doyle, members of the BSU men's and women's swim teams for their willingness to perform for the photographs; to Dr. John Reno, BSU Sport Studies Program Director, for proofreading the original manuscript; and to Mr. Dick Messner and all our colleagues at Ball State University (IN) and Winthrop College (SC) who offered support and encouragement.

CONTENTS

Section I — Introduction

Section II — Safety and First Aid

Section III — Swimming and Diving Skills

CONTENTS

CHAPTER 1
Why Learn To Swim?

The question, "Why should I learn to swim?," can be answered from several points of view. The ability to swim is essential to personal safety. It can be important in saving the life of a friend or family member. Swimming skills can be used as a physical fitness activity, as a leisure activity and as a form of therapy. Swimming ability can be a competitive activity for those who enjoy competition. Finally, the possession of swimming skills may open up many avenues of recreational activity in and around the water.

Learning to swim should be an important goal for the college student who has never had any formal training. Swimming classes in the college curriculum may offer the student one of his last opportunities to learn to swim or to improve aquatic skills. Swimming ability can be a valuable recreational asset to an individual as he enters the stressful career world. In future years, the individual may find that swimming ability is useful in the following ways:

✓ Swimming is considered to be the best fitness activity for all people. The water is a medium that allows for aerobic activity without creating stress on the body parts.

✓ The ability to swim will greatly increase the possibility for participation in a variety of new and exciting recreational activities.

✓ Parents will be able to help their own children learn to enjoy swimming and other aquatic activities.

✓ An individual who possesses some swimming skills may be able to assist the disabled and senior citizens as they participate in the aquatic environment. In this way a person can be of service to the community as a whole.

PERSONAL SAFETY

Every year more than 100 million individuals participate in aquatic activities. (2) Many of these people would be unable to either save their own lives or that of another person in case of an aquatic emergency.

Annually between 7,000 and 8,000 drownings occur in this country. (1) Sixty percent of those drownings occur in non-swimming situations. In other words, they occur from accidentally falling from docks or pool decks, from boating accidents, from fishing and ice skating accidents. In each of these situations, a non-swimmer falls into the water and is unable to remain afloat until help arrives.

Water poses a life threatening problem to those who are foolish enough to engage in activities in an aquatic environment without proper training. Individuals who live, play or work in and around the water must know how to swim well enough to save their own lives. They must also possess the ability to use basic skills to save the lives of others.

Basic swimming and rescue skills can be easily learned by anyone. They should be a prerequisite to all water activities. This would mean that an individual who engages in boating, sailing, canoeing, water skiing, surfing, snorkeling, fishing and even ice skating should be prepared to save his own life as well as assist another person who is in danger.

At some point in an individual's life, the ability to swim as well as the knowledge of a few basic rescue skills may mean the difference between life and death. No one ever knows when he may find himself or someone else in a situation that calls for immediate use of skills previously learned.

PHYSICAL FITNESS

During the past ten years, physical fitness has become an important part of the lives of millions of people. Many fitness enthusiasts have found the aquatic environment to be beneficial for all or part of their training program. (See appendix A).

Since swimming forces the heart and lungs into greater oxygen uptake and strengthens the major muscles of the body, it is an excellent activity for developing cardiovascular fitness. Swimming can be a vigorous, continuous, rhythmic activity which makes the heart beat at a rate which is high enough to produce a training effect. (3) A person who is able to stroke at a pace that raises the heart rate to 70 percent of the Heart Rate (HR) reserve level will see changes in the physical fitness level. (4)

Changes in the functioning of the cardiovascular system that can be expected from a swimming fitness program include:

1. A decrease in heart rate both at rest and during exercise, which is a result of the heart's increased ability to pump more blood with each beat.

2. A decrease in cholesterol (fatty deposits) due to an increase in high density lipoproteins (HDL) which helps eliminate cholesterol.

3. A decrease in the blood pressure brought about by a decrease in cholesterol. (3)

Swimming has a positive effect on other commonly described elements of physical fitness. It will help to improve muscle strength and endurance as well as muscle tonus. It will aid in the maintenance of flexibility of the shoulder, hip and ankle joints and the lower back. Swimming also plays an important role in the change of body composition through the loss of fat and the increase of muscle tissue. (5)

LEISURE ACTIVITY

Swimming is an enjoyable leisure activity for vast numbers of Americans who participate each year. A trip to the beach or pool on a hot summer's day would result in an awareness of the immense popularity of swimming as a leisure activity.

The popularity of swimming stems from the fact that it is an activity that can be enjoyed by people of all ages. People with varying degrees of skill can be successful participants. Because of the buoyant effect of the water, swimming is a pleasurable leisure activity that can be of benefit to individuals with various physical disabilities.

THERAPY

Water provides resistance without placing excessive stress on the muscles and joints of the body. It is not unusual for an orthopedic surgeon or physical therapist to prescribe a water exercise or activity program for those recovering from severe joint or muscle injuries.

The body's buoyancy in water makes it possible for physically handicapped individuals to participate in aquatic activities without the painful, jarring effects caused by other exercise modes. When the water temperature is raised in pools, the disabled can learn the basic skills and game activities in comfort. Swim activities are also excellent for senior citizens whose bones tend to be more brittle. There is no fear of falling because of the support provided by the water. It is one of the safest activities for the elderly.

COMPETITIVE ACTIVITIES

Once an individual possesses some swimming skills he has the necessary qualifications to participate in competitive swimming activities.

Activities include age group swimming for children and youth, interscholastic swimming for high school students and intercollegiate swimming for college students. There are even Masters swimming events for individuals of all ages beyond the typical college age.

College students who do not qualify for a collegiate team may find an opportunity for some competitive swimming through an intramural or recreational program on campus.

A relatively new competitive opportunity is in the triathlon type events and the full triathlon contest called the Iron Man. An individual who hopes to successfully compete in these events must possess good swimming skills, since the Iron Man requires a swim that is 2.4 miles in the ocean in addition to a 112 mile bike ride, and a full marathon run.

RECREATIONAL SPORTS

The ability to swim is the gateway to enjoyment of recreational swimming as well as many aquatic sports and activities. Those who have good swimming skills can, with specialized instruction, safely participate in sports such as water skiing, scuba diving, snorkeling, surfing, wind surfing, and diving.

Boating, canoeing and sailing are popular recreational aquatic sports activities. An individual who possesses some swimming skills is able to experience the pleasure of these sports without the fear of what may happen if he were suddenly thrust into the water. The recreational sports of fishing, ice fishing, and ice skating can also be safely enjoyed.

SUMMARY

Learning to swim or improving swimming skill will increase enjoyment of activities in and around the water. It may even open up new forms of leisure activities and recreational sports. Above all, swimming will provide many opportunities to live, play and work safely in and around the water.

REVIEW QUESTIONS

1. Identify three reasons why it is important to learn to swim.
2. Why is swimming considered to be an excellent activity for improving physical fitness?
3. Identify the improvements a swimming conditioning program can make to the physical functioning of the human body.
4. Why is swimming a good activity for the handicapped and the elderly?
5. Identify five water sports and activities that can be enjoyed safely by those who possess minimal swimming skills.

SELECTED REFERENCES

1. National Safety Council, (1988). *Accident Facts*. 1987. Chicago, IL: National Safety Council.
2. American National Red Cross, (1981). *Swimming and Aquatics Safety*. Washington, DC: American Red Cross.
3. Getchell, B., (1983). *Physical Fitness: A Way of Life*. New York: John Wiley and Sons.
4. Getchell, B., (1987). *The Fitness Book*. Indianapolis, IN: Benchmark Press.
5. Maglischo, E. W. & Brennan, C. F., (1985). *Swim for the Health of It*. Palo Alto, CA: Mayfield Publishing Company.

CHAPTER 2
The Story of Swimming

Swimming probably began before man recorded his activities for posterity. How the first human used the medium of water for survival, comfort and pleasure can only be conjectured. Perhaps Adam and Eve first used the Tigris-Euphrates River in the Garden of Eden for bathing, fishing and some form of recreational swimming. The first recorded swimming activities include cave drawings, mosaics and ancient bas-reliefs found in the Near East.

EARLY HISTORY OF SWIMMING

Ancient Near East

Egyptian hieroglyphics indicate evidence of some form of swimming, including lessons as early as 2500 B.C. (6) Cave drawings depicting swimmers have been found in Libya dating back to 2000 B.C. (6) Mosaics unearthed in Pompeii depict man navigating in the water, churning the hands and arms, but making little headway.

Although swimming was not included in the ancient Olympic Games, the sport dates back to early Greece and Rome. The Greeks were sailors and island inhabitants who used swimming skills for fishing and docking small craft. The Romans considered swimming an important part of their training for athletic prowess and preservation of life in time of war. (1)

Bas-reliefs show fugitives swimming across a river to a fortress while being pursued by the Assyrian army. This record, dating back to 880 B.C. shows swimmers using a stroke similar to the front crawl. (4) At times an inflated sheep or goat skin known as a "mussek" was used for support in the water. The "mussek" was braced against the body, or placed under one arm to increase buoyancy as the swimmer crossed the river with heavy armaments. (1) The *mussek* probably served as the first personal flotation device (PFD).

Europe

In Europe during the Middle Ages, monks believed in *asceticism* which refers to punishment of the body in order to elevate the spirit. Swimming for pleasure and comfort was thought to be sinful. This attitude toward swimming pervaded the societies of Europe for at least a century. (6)

Fragmentary evidence of swimming exists between the Middle Ages and the sixteenth century. The first known book on swimming was written by Nicolaus Wynman, a German, in 1538. A Latin book by Sir Everard Digby, translated into English, was published in England in 1587. (2)

A little over a hundred years later, in 1697, a Frenchman named Thevenot wrote *The Art of Swimming.* (2) He described a stroke similar to the breaststroke that had already been used for many years. The English translated this book to use for a standard reference in schools and libraries. The British Museum contains numerous archaeological artifacts and proof texts from literature authenticating swimming activity and the first forms of strokes used by mankind. The word "swimming" comes from the old English "swimmin" and established the English people as the first to make a sport out of the various stroke forms used to propel the body in water. (8)

Japan

Japan is the country in which competitive swimming events originated. The first recorded swimming competition occurred during the reign of Emperor Suigiu in 36 B.C. (3) Much later, in 1603, the Japanese made swimming compulsory in the schools, and instituted the first inter-school meets. (7)

MODERN HISTORY OF SWIMMING

Nineteenth Century

By 1837 there were several indoor pools constructed in England. (5) Soon after swimming competition began in London. Contests were governed by the National Swimming Society in England. In 1844 some American Indians went to London for the purpose of competing in swimming. Flying Gull defeated Tobacco, his friend, by swimming the length of a 130 foot pool in 30 seconds, thereby winning a medal. London newspapers described the stroke used by the American Indians as "thrashing water violently with arms rotating out of the water like sails of a windmill, beating the feet downward, and blowing out forcefully". (8) The English rejected this form of the crawl preferring to stay with the breaststroke for many years.

After watching the South American Indians swim, Englishman John Trudgen (sometimes spelled "Trudgeon") returned to England in 1862 with an idea for a new stroke. (8) It consisted of an overarm movement combined with a scissors kick. This stroke, which caught on, is known as the *trudgen stroke* and is still used today.

Swimming the English Channel was first accomplished by Captain Matthew Webb of England in 1875 using a breaststroke. Swimmers continue to challenge the Channel to this day. In 1983, Ashby Harper became the oldest swimmer to complete the Channel swim. He was 65 years, 362 days old at the time. (10)

At the end of the nineteenth century, with competitive meets on the increase, there was a need to streamline strokes for greater speed. Attention was redirected from arm movements to leg movements.

Twentieth Century

The Australian crawl (also called the American crawl, front crawl, or freestyle) was introduced by Richard Cavill in 1902. At the International Championships, he used it to swim 100 yards in 58.4 seconds for a new world record. (2) This marked the beginning of a new era in speed swimming.

During the 1920's the Japanese made extensive use of slow-motion films. The strokes of Olympic medalist Johnny Weismuller and other great swimmers were studied. These films allowed teachers and coaches to help students improve their stroke mechanics.

The inverted breaststroke was invented in the early 1900's. The body was turned over from the breaststroke front lying (prone) position to a back lying (supine) position in the water. A new stroke was created by performing basically the same movements as in the breaststroke while on the back.

Not long afterwards (1912), the front crawl was inverted to create a stroke called the back crawl (also called the backstroke). It was immediately favored for competition over the breaststroke because of its speed. (2)

In 1934, David Armbruster, a university swimming coach, created a variation of the breaststroke using a simultaneous double arm recovery over the water. A year later, this variation was used with a dolphin kick and the stroke came to be known as the butterfly.

For 20 years, the dolphin kick was disallowed in competition and a shortened breaststroke kick was required. Early in the 1950's the dolphin was finally legalized for competition. The breaststroke and butterfly, as we know them today, became separate strokes. (2)

Whether these basic strokes are performed for recreation or for competition, our forefathers have created swimming strokes that are effective for propelling the human body through the water. It is possible that there are more efficient ways to swim. It is up to those who live today and those who will live in the future to improve current strokes or create new strokes for recreation or competition.

ROLE OF SWIMMING IN INTERNATIONAL SPORTS

Olympic Games

Swimming was included when the modern Olympic Games were first instituted in Athens in 1896. There were four events of which three were for men's freestyle. The fourth was a race for sailors on ships anchored in the port where the Olympic races were held.

Women were not included in the first three Olympic Games. They were also not allowed to attend because the races were conducted in the nude. Coubertin, the French inventor of the modern Games, resisted efforts to include women for 10 years. Women competed first in the 1912 Olympics (Stockholm) at the suggestion of the International Federation which is known today as the *International Olympic Committee* (IOC). (12)

The sport has remained in the summer Olympic Games ever since its first appearance. In the early Olympiads there were some strange events. At the second Olympics (1900) in Paris three events were held which have not been repeated. There was an obstacle race where competitors had to climb over a pole, maneuver over a row of boats, and then swim under a row of boats. Another event was an underwater swimming endurance contest. The longest swimming event was also held which was 4000 meters. In 1904, a long distance plunging championship was held for the first and only time.

As the Games and the sport developed, more events were added, and standards were established. By the 1972 Olympics in Munich, 29 swimming races were held, 15 for men and 14 for women. These standardized races or events continue to be held in the modern day Olympic Games. (4)

International Competition for the Handicapped

The Comite International des Sports des Sourds (CISS) is the oldest international organization which offers sporting competition for the disabled. In 1924, CISS held the first Summer World Games for the deaf. The Games included swimming events for both men and women.

The first opportunity for mentally retarded athletes to participate in international competition occurred in the summer of 1968. Swimming was included in the First International Special Olympics Games which were held in Chicago. In the 1983 International Summer Special Olympic Games, competition was held in diving plus six men's swimming events and six women's swimming events. (11)

Today there are many opportunities for the disabled to compete in swimming activities. Additional organizations have been established which make it possible for the blind, the paraplegic and those with other locomotor disabilities (i.e. cerebral palsy and multiple sclerosis) to successfully compete in international swimming events.

REVIEW QUESTIONS

1. What existing evidence leads us to believe that swimming skills were used more than 2000 years B.C.?

2. What factors have made the greatest impact on improving competitive swimming times at various distances during the twentieth century?

3. What is the most recently developed competitive swimming stroke? Who developed it? When? How long has it been used in competition?

4. Why were women excluded from Olympic swimming competition until 1912?

5. What opportunities do disabled individuals have for international competition in swimming?

SELECTED REFERENCES

1. American National Red Cross. (1956). *Lifesaving and Water Safety*. Garden City, NY: Doubleday.

2. American National Red Cross. (1981). *Swimming and Aquatic Safety*. Washington, DC: American Red Cross.

3. Anderson, B., (ed.) (1975). *Sportsource*. Mountain View, CA: World Publications.

4. Arlott, J., (ed.) (1975). *The Oxford Companions to World Sports and Games.* London, England: Oxford University Press.

5. Hickok, R., (ed.) (1977). *New Encyclopedia of Sports.* New York, NY: McGraw-Hill.

6. Hovis, F., (ed.) (1976). *The Sports Encyclopedia.* New York, NY: Praeger.

7. Oppenheim, F., (1970). *The History of Swimming.* North Hollywood, CA: Swimming World.

8. Menke, F. G. & Palmer, P., (1978). *The Encyclopedia of Sports.* (6th ed.) Southbrunswick, New York: A.S. Barnes.

9. Morris, D., (1969). *Swimming.* London, England: Heinemann Educational Books, Ltd.

10. Russell, A., (ed.) (1987). *1988 Guinness Book of World Records.* New York, NY: Sterling.

11. Sherrill, C., (ed.) (1986). *Sport and Disabled Athletes. The 1984 Olympic Scientific Congress Proceedings.* Vol. 9. Champaign, IL: Human Kinetics.

12. Spears, B. and Swanson, R.A., (1983). *History of Sport and Physical Activity in the United States.* Dubuque, IA: Wm. C. Brown.

CHAPTER 3
Use of Aquatic Equipment and Supplies

Swimming, like many other sports, has advanced to the point where there are a number of companies making equipment for class and competitive use. New equipment and variations of old equipment are constantly being developed to improve swimming techniques and to make the sport more enjoyable. A number of manufacturers and suppliers of aquatic equipment have been listed in appendix B.

Equipment used by the swimmer includes: a swim suit, a sweat suit, a mask, fins, and snorkel. Useful swimming supplies include: earplugs, nose plugs, goggles, kick boards and pulling devices. Many swimmers also use swim caps, a swimming chamois, bath sheets and various flotation devices. Swimming pool lifts are large pieces of equipment available to help disabled students get in and out of the water. Some pools are equipped with ramps which allow easy entrance and exit for disabled students.

This chapter will acquaint the student with the various types of equipment and supplies that are available. It will help the student become aware of the cost, proper use and care of items used in typical college or university settings.

SWIMWEAR

Swimsuits

Unlike swimsuits of yesteryear, today's suits are scientifically designed. New fabrics and styles help to cut down water resistance. This allows an individual to swim faster.

Today's suits come in several choices of fabric. These include nylon and stretch nylon under such trade names as *Lycra, Copel,* and *Miraculon.* Women's one piece nylon suits are preferred for class purposes. They come in a multitude of designs and colors. The nylon suit is most suitable because of its strength, durability, snag resistance and fast drying qualities. Most women's suits range in price from $20.00 to $40.00.

For class purposes, men's full cut nylon suits with elasticized, draw-string waist and full front lining are appropriate. Many men prefer the boxer style swimsuit in various lengths for recreational and class use.

Care should be taken in selecting a color in a nylon suit. Red's and white's have a tendency to become transparent when they are wet. If those colors are chosen, be sure that the suit has an extra layer of fabric (double panel) in the front.

No matter what style of suit or type of material is chosen, proper care is important. Always rinse out the swimsuit in clear, fresh water immediately after swimming, or take a soap shower with it on. It should also be wrung out and hung up to dry. Proper care will increase the life of the suit.

Sweatsuits

Sweatsuits are often worn over swimsuits during part of the swimming class. Jackets are also worn immediately after emerging from the water if subsequent entry into the water is delayed. This may happen frequently when watching demonstrations of strokes by the instructor in class.

SWIMMING SUPPLIES

Earplugs

Some swimmers are prone to ear problems due to water which gets into the ears and remains there. Earplugs may solve the problem. However, use of the tiny, pre-formed earplugs found in many drugstores should be avoided. One man used these and when he finished swimming, he was unable to remove one earplug. All efforts to remove it failed. Several days later, a doctor removed it. The result was a very sore, infected ear, and an expensive doctor bill.

If it is necessary to prevent water from entering the ears, the swimmer has several options. Wax earplugs may be used. These easily conform to the individual ear and do a good job of keeping water out. Another product that can be molded to fit any ear is the silicone earplug. Either the wax or silicone plugs are comfortable and do not irritate the ear. They can be used by most individuals. These are inexpensive and available at sporting goods stores. If these products do not work satisfactorily, visit an ear specialist who can mold plugs that will alleviate the problem.

Noseplugs

Many swimming instructors do not encourage the use of noseplugs. This is particularly true at the beginning level of swimming. It is essential that a swimmer not become dependent upon noseplugs. Falling into the water could cause panic in a swimmer who has never learned to swim without noseplugs.

Some competitive swimmers use noseclips when swimming the backstroke. They are also widely used in synchronized swimming.

Rubber noseplugs with an attached headband are available in many drugstores and sporting goods stores. Plastic covered, wire noseclips in several sizes can be found in shops that specialize in swimming equipment.

Goggles

Goggles can be used to protect the eyes from chlorinated water as well as to improve vision underwater. They come in a variety of styles and colors. Most goggles have a leakproof seal

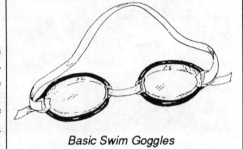

Basic Swim Goggles

made of rubber or some other hypo-allergenic material. Before purchasing a pair of goggles, make sure that they fit properly. Proper fit ensures that they will not leak during use.

Water Sox

Water sox or low-cut rubber boots are available in vivid colors wherever water equipment items are sold. They are most useful for SCUBA, but can be used in aquarobics classes or for sensitive feet in all swimming classes.

Kickboards

Kickboards are important pieces of equipment for anyone who takes swimming seriously. They are used by the novice to learn the kick and by the expert to develop a strong kick. They come in a variety of colorful lightweight materials. The most commonly used kickboards are made of styrofoam. They are approximately 22" x 12" x 1" with one rounded end.

To properly use the kickboard for the basic strokes on the front (crawl or breaststroke), hold the kickboard out in front of the body at arms length and place the hands on the corners of the board. Press down on the board hard enough to cause the rounded end to ride slightly out of the water.

Use of kickboards in back and prone positions

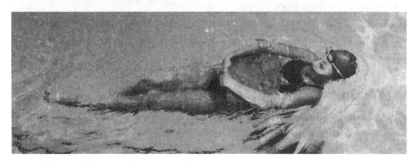

For strokes on the back (elementary backstroke or back crawl), lie on the back while holding the kickboard. One technique is performed by using both hands to extend the board behind the head while keeping the elbows straight. A second technique is executed by holding the board on top of the body across the abdomen. The arms rest on top of the board, and hold it in place.

Although modern kickboards are made to last, they should not be abused. Do not stand on them, throw them or slap the water with them.

Left to right: pullbuoy, kickboard, and hand paddle (training paddle)

PULLING DEVICES

Hand Paddles

A number of different implements have been devised to wear on the hands to practice the pulling action of the arm stroke. Hand paddles are the most frequently used and are the least expensive of these pulling devices. Swimmers use hand paddles to develop proper form in strokes, strength and speed.

In order to avoid tendonitis of the elbow, most individuals should use either a small or medium sized hand paddle. Injuries can also be avoided by limiting their initial use to short distances.

Pull Buoys

A pull buoy is a device used to keep the legs afloat without kicking. The pull buoy allows the swimmer to concentrate on arm action. Most pull buoys are composed of two 6" to 8" long cylinder shaped pieces of styrofoam held together by an adjustable nylon cord.

For proper use, the pull buoy should be held between the thighs. One of the cylinders should be on top and one below the legs. The size (6", 7" or 8") of the pull buoy is determined by leg length, amount of buoyancy needed and comfort.

PT "Trainer Tube"

Another device that has recently been developed to help the swimmer concentrate on his stroke is the PT *trainer tube*. The PT tube is an inflatable rubber ring. It comes in a 4", 6" or 8" size.

PT tubes provide buoyancy for the legs as well as drag for the body. An advantage of the PT tube is that buoyancy and resistance can be adjusted by inflating or deflating the tube.

The 4" tube is used around the ankles. The 6" tube is placed around the lower legs. The 8" tubes are twisted and used around the ankles or lower legs. Novices should not use these tubes, since they may have difficulty freeing their feet to stand up when necessary.

UNDERWATER EQUIPMENT

The mask, fins and snorkel are used by many swimmers for recreational purposes. Snorkeling is an enjoyable activity which allows the swimmer to more fully appreciate the wonders of marine life. Scuba diving is also a popular activity. It too can be used to enjoy the aquatic environment as well as for search and rescue operations.

As with most equipment, there is a variety of styles to choose from. The swimmer who is interested in purchasing equipment for snorkeling or for scuba diving should go to a dive shop to discuss his particular needs with a qualified expert. Dive shops are usually owned and operated by scuba instructors who are knowledgeable about equipment.

It is not necessary to purchase the most expensive, elaborate equipment to be able to enjoy the sport. However, there are certain characteristics of good equipment that an individual should look for when making a purchase. Since the characteristics are specific to each piece of equipment, they will be identified in the following discussion of mask, fins and snorkel.

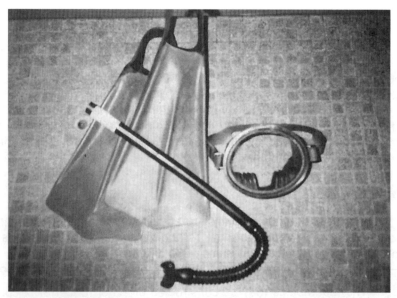

Mask with fingerpockets, fins, and snorkel with corrugated tubing at bottom

Mask

When purchasing a face mask, be sure that its face-piece is composed of tempered glass which is held in place by a corrosion resistant metal band. The skirt of the mask should fit the face and be made of soft, flexible silicone. Inexpensive plastic or rubber masks are not recommended for use by small children or for recreational purposes.

Optional features include a purge valve, a nose pocket and finger pockets. Purge valves for the mask are questionable due to leakage and the intrusion of debris. The nose pocket and/or finger pocket enables the user to easily equalize pressure in the ears. This is an important option to a swimmer who makes deep dives.

For safe use, the mask should not be placed over the mouth. Do not dive from the deck with the mask on. Proper techniques for entering the water while wearing the mask should be learned and used.

Before putting a mask on, wash it with water or place a few drops of glycerine on it to prevent fogging. Do not use saliva to defog the mask. The practice of spitting in the mask could cause eye infections. Place the mask snugly against the face with one hand. Use the other hand to secure the strap behind the head.

Fins

Fins come in a variety of sizes and styles. A prospective buyer should look for proper fit, flexibility and appropriate blade size. A beginner should use fins which have blades that are approximately equal to the length of his foot.

Fins may have either a full shoe foot or a foot pocket with a heel strap. The full foot type is prone to tear at the heel and cannot be repaired. The heel strap style is preferred since broken straps are replaceable and they allow for foot growth. An option that may be important is whether or not they float.

Professional diving fins are made of silicone. Before purchasing a pair of fins, make sure that they fit properly. Try them on with bare feet. A slightly loose fit is better than one that is too tight. Tight fins may cause leg cramps.

Snorkel

Snorkels are L or J-shaped rubber tubes used for breathing while the face is under water. Rigidly constructed ones are not recommended. Those constructed with a corrugated portion at the bottom of the "J" are best. The mouthpiece may be constructed of either rubber or silicone. The lip guards and teeth lugs should fit the individual.

Snorkels made of silicone with a one inch diameter tube, and with a purge valve at the bottom of the "J" are most efficient for snorkeling. The large bore tube allows for a greater air exchange and a quicker clearing of water from the tube. The purge valve also facilitates clearing of the tube.

The snorkel should come with a strap hanger or a "keeper" that attaches to the mask. The "keeper" is used to hold the snorkel in the correct position in relation to the mask.

Masks, fins and snorkels which are properly cared for will last for many years. Rinse them thoroughly in clear water after each use. This is particularly important when using them in chlorinated pool water.

MISCELLANEOUS EQUIPMENT AND SUPPLIES

Chair-Lift

Several companies have produced a device known as a chair-lift or a pool-lift. This device is used to assist disabled individuals in entering and exiting the water. The chair lift is an expensive piece of equipment which is permanently anchored to the pool deck. To use the lift, the disabled individual sits in a special chair or a sling which is lowered into the water by use of a hand crank. One company produces a lift that is designed to be operated by the disabled individual or by an assistant. Pressure from a garden hose produces the lifting power.

Hoyer Pool Lift

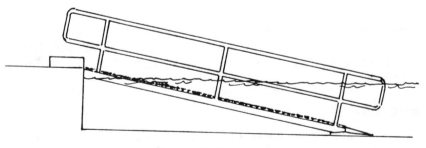

Removable Access Ramp

Ramps

Ramps are devices which allow a disabled person to walk into or out of the pool. They are designed with a gradual slope from the deck to the pool bottom. Double handrails are fitted to them so that the disabled person can walk down into the pool unassisted. Ramps can either be purchased from a number of manufacturers or constructed locally. Playing on or near the ramp should be discouraged.

Swimcaps

Although swimcaps were once used only by women, today's caps are worn by members of both sexes. The traditional chin strap cap is constructed of heavyweight rubber and offers women the best protection against wetness. Generally caps are not required in swimming classes. However, caps may be required for those with long hair at some private and public pools. Racing style caps worn by both men and women are made of latex, silicon, or lycra. The latex and silicon caps help to keep the hair dry. The main purpose of the lycra cap is to keep the hair in place and to cut down on water resistance, since it will not keep the hair dry. Caps of all varieties are found at most sporting goods outlets.

Chamois and Other Towels

A new product being used by many swimmers is a small (17" x 13") soft, poly-vinyl towel. This "towel" works like a chamois to absorb water quickly. It can be used over and over to dry the swimmer who must get in and out of the water frequently. Two such products are known by such registered trade names as "The Sammy" and the "Speedo Chamois."

Although the chamois is increasing in use, the good old-fashioned terrycloth towel is still used. The towel comes in handy as a convenient warm wrap. It is also used to roll a wet suit, cap and/or goggles up to carry them around campus. Toss the small bundle into a backpack or clip it under the back carrier of a bike for convenience.

Giant towels that cover almost the whole body are called bath sheets and readily available. They are bulky for a backpack, but they are warm when used after a refreshing, brisk swim. They are ideal for classes in which it is necessary to go in and out of the water repeatedly. They are also favored for outdoor swimming.

SUMMARY

Today's aquatics enthusiast may select from a wide range of equipment and supplies to enhance his enjoyment and improve his skills. Modern technology has been used to improve upon older items and to develop new equipment and supplies.

Swimmers have a wide selection of suits available to them in sleek styles, bright colors and low friction fabrics. They can wear colorful caps to keep their hair dry or to keep it pulled back. They can protect their eyes, ears and nose from irritation caused by the water. When they are ready to get out of the water they can quickly dry off with a miniature or giant towel.

Special equipment is available to practice various parts of the stroke. Swimmers can also choose equipment that meets their specific needs for underwater swimming sports in which they have an interest.

Equipment has been developed to give pool access to the disabled individual for learning new skills in the water. Two such pieces of equipment, the chair-lift and the ramp, have made it much easier for the disabled individual to get in and out of the water, thereby increasing enjoyment.

REVIEW QUESTIONS

1. What characteristics should be considered when selecting a mask? Fins? Snorkel? ⎯⎯

2. What options are available to an individual who continually gets water in his ears?

3. What is the proper method of using a kickboard when kicking on the back?

4. Why should an individual learn to swim without noseplugs?

5. What devices are available for use in practicing the arm strokes? How would each be used?

SELECTED REFERENCES

1. American National Red Cross. (1968). *Lifesaving and Water Safety Courses.* Instructor's Manual. Washington, DC: American Red Cross.

2. American National Red Cross. (1974). *Lifesaving Rescue and Water Safety.* Garden City, NY: Doubleday.

3. American National Red Cross. (1981). *Swimming and Aquatics Safety.* Garden City, NY: Doubleday.

4. Brown, T. & Hunter, R., (1978). *Concise Book of Snorkeling.* Agincourt, Canada: Gage Publishing.

CHAPTER 4
Safe Conduct In Water Environments

To the non-swimmer, a body of water, whether a lake or pool, can be a serious threat, something to be avoided. Why? Because he fears drowning. To the swimmer, water is an enjoyable environment. Why? Because he anticipates fun, recreation, and relaxation.

Classes in which swimming skills are taught are actually "water safety courses". The term, "water safety", implies that skills and knowledges will be taught to help the student gain confidence in his ability to safely participate in all types of water environments.

Safety in and around the water necessitates compliance with a commonly accepted set of safety rules. Knowledge and understanding as well as adherence to those rules of safety will reduce the incidence of accidents. Let's look at some principles and illustrations along with the safety rules that accompany them.

SAFETY PRINCIPLES, ILLUSTRATIONS AND RULES

1. Know how close to go to the water's edge.

Children often tumble into pools, lakes or rivers trying to retrieve a leaf, a lost toy, or any attractive item. Fishing along steep banks may precipitate a sudden fall into a swirling river. In either case, falling into the water may cause drowning. If the victim is wearing heavy clothing, survival is less likely.

RULE: Carefully supervise children when they are near the water.

RULE: Stay away from the water's edge when fully clothed.

2. Know the water depth when swimming or boating.

It is not uncommon to be swimming and step down only to find that the bottom is not there. At other times, inexperienced swimmers can be easily lured into deep water by swimming after friends or desired objects such as a beach ball, an air bed or a rubber tube which is carried by the wind or current. Novice swimmers caught in these situations may panic.

Water depth is also an important factor in diving. Individuals are frequently injured by diving into water that is too shallow. It is very foolish to dive into water if you do not know the depth or the condition of the bottom. This may cause injuries to the fingers and hands as well as to the head, neck and back. Unfortunately, there are many paraplegic and quadriplegic individuals in wheelchairs today because of diving accidents.

> RULE: *Swimmers should avoid using free floating objects that may be carried away by water or the wind.*

> RULE: *If caught in deep water, stay calm and turn toward shore, level off and begin to propel your body to a safe depth.*

> RULE: *Water depth should be a minimum of five feet for a head first dive to be attempted.*

3. Know that diving into deep water or swimming vigorously after a full meal may be life threatening.

A young man at a summer camp ate a big lunch of macaroni and cheese. Soon afterwards he dived into deep water but never came up. Autopsy results showed that he had regurgitated, and the stomach contents were aspirated into his lungs.

Swimming after a light snack may cause no discomfort, however, strenuous swimming soon after a heavy meal may cause abdominal discomfort. Although everyone has heard that they should not go swimming for at least an hour after eating in order to prevent stomach cramps, there is no basis for this warning. As in the example above, recent studies have confirmed that individuals have died from aspirating vomitus rather than from stomach cramps.

Fortunately, most people do not want to participate in vigorous activities for an hour or more after eating. Most adults react to the discomfort and get out of the water. However, young children must be closely supervised, since they have a tendency to ignore discomfort while playing.

> RULE: *Wait at least one hour after eating a heavy meal before diving or participating in vigorous swimming activities.*

4. Know that swimming with others is safer than swimming alone.

It may seem very relaxing to go out for a swim alone, but it is not wise. An engaged couple was swimming on a crowded beach. The young lady left for a few moments to visit the restroom. When she returned, her fiance had disappeared from the end of the pier where she had left him. Failing to find him she urged the lifeguard to join the search. Within minutes, the young man was found near the end of the pier in 14 feet of water. Attempts to revive him failed. No one knows what caused the drowning, but had they followed the "buddy system" used in summer camps, he may be alive today. Swimming with a "buddy" is the best safety system known today. Good swimmers often overestimate their abilities and attempt to swim unaccompanied across lakes. A number of them never make it to the other side.

RULE: Never swim alone.

RULE: Use the "buddy system" when swimming. Stay close to a friend. Be within sight of each other at all times. If you must leave, have the other person sit on the deck or pier until you return.

RULE: Never attempt to swim across a lake unless accompanied by an individual in a boat.

5. Know the extent of your swimming ability, have a healthy fear of the water.

Over-confidence in swimming ability or in the use of small craft may result in an accident. Individuals who have spent a great deal of time in and around the water frequently lose what would be considered a "healthy fear" of the water. They become careless and may fail to practice common sense rules for safety.

Several years ago, a young robust lifeguard finished a long hot day on the beach and joined his friends in a speedboat. Although he knew better, he sat on the gunwales (sides) of the boat. The boat driver suddenly swerved to avoid another boat. The lifeguard was thrown into the water and fatally cut by the outboard motor blades.

RULE: Use good common sense in and around the water and avoid dangerous activities that may lead to injury.

6. Know your rescue and resuscitation capabilities.

It is foolish to swim after a friend in trouble unless you are a qualified lifeguard and have first attempted all other means of rescue. Untrained individuals could use a pole, broom, towel or anything available in the vicinity of the water to extend the reach. Other options for the untrained swimmer would include throwing a device such as a ring buoy or using a boat to help a swimmer who is in trouble. Indviduals who spend time in and around the water should learn rescue breathing and CPR. They should also take the time to practice these skills periodically so that they are ready to use them, in case of an emergency.

> RULE: Learn all the skills needed to effect proper rescue and resuscitation techniques. Enroll in an American Red Cross CPR course today.

7. Know the fallibility of air-filled flotation devices.

Inflatable devices such as inner tubes, air mattresses, beach balls and other toys are always a safety hazard. This is especially true at crowded beaches.

Parents as well as children frequently gain a false sense of security when inflatable devices are used. Because parents feel safe, they fail to supervise small children whom they feel are "protected" by inflatable objects. Small children, weak swimmers and even non-swimmers use inflatable devices to venture into deep water. Falling off the object, losing hold of the object or an air leak places the user in a life threatening situation.

Water wings used by children or disabled individuals provide buoyancy and are beneficial in learning to swim. Instructors and students must realize that these flotation devices are only temporary and are subject to deflation and detachment. Canister type floats can be dangerous. They are not designed to keep the face of an unconscious person out of the water. Therefore, close supervision of their use is necessary.

> RULE: Limit the use of flotation devices by novices to times when they are under the direct supervision of an adult.

8. Know that horseplay and false alarms are dangerous.

Having fun while playing recreational water games should stop short of dangerous practices which may cause injury or fear. Some examples of dangerous practices include: pushing someone into deep water, jerking a person's arm down to pull them under the water and holding someone's head under the water repeatedly.

Another dangerous practice involves distracting the lifeguard by pretending to be in trouble. Swimmers should avoid thrashing around in the water as if they were about to drown and yelling for help when assistance is not needed. These activities may draw the attention of the lifeguard away from an actual life-threatening situation.

> RULE: *Play water games that do not include elements of injury, fear, or potential drowning.*

> RULE: *Never yell "help" or draw the attention of the lifeguard when assistance is not needed.*

9. Know that swimming at an unsupervised beach is hazardous.

The only safe place to swim is at an established beach where there are lifeguards who have been trained to handle emergencies that may arise.

Several years ago, a family arrived at a beach in a Pennsylvania State Park that was closed because of extremely rough water. They refused to accept the fact that they would not be able to go swimming that day. They went to another area of beach that was not used for swimming because of the dangers associated with the retaining wall. Not long after entering the water, the eight year old son was impaled on a spike located below the water level. The force of the waves caused the spike to be driven further and further into his body. The young man was helpless, and his family was helpless in their attempts to rescue the boy. Authorities knew of the dangers that existed in this area of the beach. That is why NO SWIMMING ALLOWED signs were posted.

> RULE: *Never swim in an area that is marked NO SWIMMING.*

> RULE: *Never swim at a beach that has been temporarily closed because of weather conditions or potential danger to swimmers.*

10. Know common health hazards around water, their prevention and care.

a. **Blue lips and fingernails and shivering** are signs of lowered body temperature and possible hypothermia.

> RULE: *Keep active. It is best to get out of the water and wrap up in a warm dry towel.*

b. **Walking on sharp, slippery, moss covered rocks** which are located under the water causes cuts to the feet and may cause broken bones upon falling.

RULE: To prevent injury wear gym shoes with rubber soles when in water with a rocky bottom.

c. **High humidity and hot temperatures,** even on a cloudy day, may cause first and second degree sunburn.

RULE: For prevention wear sunscreen oils or lotions and wear light colored clothes and bathing suits. Do not fall asleep unprotected on the beach. Do not stay in the water more than two hours on a hot day.

FIRST AID: Use cold cloths or compresses for first degree burns. Lanolin rich lotions may help to reduce pain. For second degree sunburn (when small blisters appear) place cold, wet towels on the affected area. Follow by covering with dry dressings. Do not use lotions or salves. In the case of sun poisoning, take aspirin, get bed rest and seek medical aid, if needed.

AQUATIC ENVIRONMENTS

Each type of aquatic environment has its own hazards. Therefore, it is necessary to consider specific safety guidelines for pools, fresh water, and salt water facilities.

Pools

Potentially hazardous areas in institutional and commercial pools would include locker rooms, decks and diving areas. Health and safety guidelines for each of these areas should include:

Locker Rooms

1. Be careful when moving near sharp edges of open lockers.
2. Shower before entering the pool area.
3. Keep cosmetics in non-breakable, protective containers.
4. Towel dry in the shower area in order to help eliminate wet slippery floors in the locker room.
5. Do not use electric dryers or curling irons when standing barefoot on wet floors.
6. Keep the feet clean and dry to avoid athlete's feet and other fungus problems.
7. Use sauna and whirlpool facilities properly after medical approval.

Decks

1. Refrain from running.
2. Do not bring glass containers of any kind onto the deck.
3. Avoid stepping on pool or lifesaving equipment such as flutter boards, pull buoys, ring buoys, or rescue tubes.
4. Do not enter the water if a lifeguard is not present.
5. Do not sunbathe near the edge of the pool.
6. Do not climb on lifeguard chairs or play with emergency equipment.

Diving Areas

1. Always be sure that the area beneath the board is free of objects or individuals before jumping or diving into the pool.
2. Always jump off an unfamiliar board before diving off of it. This should be done in order to determine water depth and the characteristics of the board.
3. Only one diver should be on the board at a time.
4. Do not attempt difficult dives unless you have had instruction in how to perform them.
5. Dive only from the end of the board, and be sure to dive straight out from the board (that's where the pool is deepest).
6. Do not take several bounces on the end of the board prior to jumping or diving.
7. Swim to the side as quickly as possible after finishing the dive.
8. Do not hang on the boards.
9. Do not swim in the areas directly under or in front of the diving boards.

Fresh Water

Lakes and rivers pose a unique set of problems. These problems can be overcome by following a few simple safety guidelines.

✓ When tangled in weeds, don't panic. Use slow, gentle, back and forth movements of the limbs to become free of them.

✓ Stay far from dangerous river currents. Rescue may require assistance.

✓ Avoid swimming near fallen trees, large rocks, or wrecks which could cause currents.

✓ Swim in line with the shore or river bank.

✓ At guarded beaches, swim only in the area that has been marked off for swimming.

✓ Do not swim at a beach that has been closed because of weather or water conditions.

✓ Water snakes will not attack if you stay calm, wait until they pass and continue cautiously. If bitten, slowly swim ashore. Treat the bite as an insect bite if the snake was a non-poisonous variety. If bitten by a water moccasin, apply ice and get anti-venom serum from the nearest poison control center. Police may need to be contacted for assistance.

Salt Water

Ocean swimming and surfing have dangers that are inherent to the environment. Procedures to follow when swimming and surfing in the ocean include the following:

✓ Do not use rhythmic breathing in salt water for any length of time. Nose and throat passages will become irritated. Breath with the head out of the water.

✓ Swimming in high waves will cause difficulty in breathing unless each wave is anticipated and breathing regulated.

✓ Stay within 50 feet of shore to avoid the uncertainty of under-currents, surf dangers, and large water mammals lurking in shallow waters.

✓ After a storm, jellyfish and Portuguese man-of-war marine animals often drift ashore. Because they look like clear balloons on the water, children are prone to pick them up. The tentacles discharge venom which produces immediate pain, and causes a rash with minute hemorrhages in the skin. If a large area of skin is affected, particularly near the face; shock, muscle cramps, vomiting and respiratory difficulty or death may result. The very young as well as the old and infirmed are particularly vulnerable to adverse reactions. Rub the affected area immediately with wet sand, then apply diluted ammonia or rubbing alcohol. Bed rest, aspirin, or medical aid may be needed.

✓ Swim only at beaches designated for swimming.

AQUATIC SPORTS

Water sports occupy great amounts of time and cost millions of American recreational enthusiasts a great deal of money. In order to thoroughly enjoy these sports, safe habits must be established, and risk taking reduced to a minimum. The following precautions should be considered when participating in water skiing, using small craft, snorkeling or scuba diving.

Water Skiing

Water skiing requires a well-trained boat driver for stopping, starting, and avoiding other craft. A certified personal flotation device (PFD) or ski belt must be worn by the skier. Never take off from a pier. Establish signals between the skier and boat driver for speeding up, slowing down, taking the skier to shore, and stopping. Have a certified lifeguard, if possible, on the ski boat. It is also important to have one or more observers in the boat to ensure the safety of the skier.

Small Craft

The use of small craft such as rowboats, canoes, and sailboats causes special concerns. One particular danger can be the wake of a ski boat that causes swamping or overturning of small craft. It is best to turn the bow (front) of the boat so that it is at a right angle to the wake.

If a storm is anticipated, head for shore. The calm before a storm is a good warning signal to go in. If a sailboat does not get to shore before the "calm" it can be caught "in irons" (or unable to move because of no wind) and often has to bear the brunt of a heavy downpour. Carry a paddle or two in the sailboat for such an emergency.

All occupants of boats must wear, or at least carry, a Coast Guard approved PFD on board. Ski belts do not qualify as approved PFD's because a person hit in the head by a ski may be suspended face down in the water. Canoe users must be particularly knowledgeable about maneuvering around currents and waterfalls, as well as circumventing other dangerous objects, especially in white water rivers.

Snorkeling and Scuba Diving

Snorkeling and scuba diving are growing in their popularity as water sports. Scuba diving is not only a good recreational activity, but it is also being widely used for ice and submerged vehicle rescue. As the number of participants increases, the incidence of accidents also increases. Well made equipment and adequate training for its use are absolutely essential for safety below the water. Those vacationing in the south sea islands need to be particularly aware of underwater caves, currents and coral reefs just beneath the surface of the water. Completing a scuba class with a qualified instructor will give a person skills not only for leisure time enjoyment but for water rescue assistance when needed in the community.

Ice Activities

Many who live in northern climates enjoy a variation in their aquatic activities during the winter months. Solid water (ice) can provide recreational opportunities for the young and the old. Enthusiasts take to the ice to engage in skating, hockey, sledding, sailing, snowmobiling as well as ice boating and ice fishing. Since a body of water is involved, none of these activities is entirely without danger.

Venturing onto unsafe ice can be a nemesis for young and old alike. Children love to slide or sled on ice after school. Alvaro Garza, age 11, was sledding with his brother Joey when he fell through thin ice near his home in Moorhead, Minnesota. Four years earlier, Terrence Tontlewicz, age 5, was also sledding and slipped beneath the icy waters of Lake Michigan. Both boys miraculously survived with minimal brain damage after more that 20 minutes in icy waters. Unfortunately, many children caught in the same circumstances do not survive.

Adults can lose their lives in late winter by slipping through thin ice while ice fishing. Others drown when skating, walking or snowmobiling across unsafe ice.

Many accidents could be avoided by following a few simple safety rules. Never venture onto thin ice. Ice thickness should be at least two inches for children and three inches for adults. A good rule of thumb to follow in relation to ice thickness is to wait until the temperature has been 20 degrees or less for at least three consecutive days before engaging in ice activities. Late in the season ice that looks firm may be very soft. Stay off the ice once the temperatures begin to rise near the freezing point.

SUMMARY

Each type of aquatic environment or activity has a unique set of characteristics that affect its potential for accidents. It is the responsibility of the participant to make himself aware of the hazards related to the facility or activity. He must then take the necessary precautions to ensure his own safety as well as the safety of others.

Aquatics enthusiasts should prepare themselves to safely participate in their favorite activities by taking specialized training in lifesaving techniques, first aid and CPR, while also learning how to properly use equipment, learning how to swim, or taking courses in boating, sailing, canoeing, scuba diving and water skiing.

There are several organizations that provide courses designed to make individuals safe in and around the water. Included among these organizations are the following:

- The American Red Cross which offers classes in swimming, lifeguard training, first aid, CPR, and small craft safety.

- The YMCA which offers classes in swimming and lifesaving.

- The Coast Guard which is prepared to teach the rudiments of safety in the use of of all types of boats.

- PADI, a regulatory body for the teaching of scuba diving, offers training courses for beginners as well as those who would like to become instructors.

- Universities and colleges offer a wide range of aquatic activities within the physical education curriculum. Courses taught frequently include: swimming, lifesaving, WSI, first aid, CPR, canoeing, sailing and scuba diving.

Take advantage of the community organizations which are prepared to help aquatic participants become more knowledgeable about how to safely participate in their favorite activities.

REVIEW QUESTIONS

1. Children love to play in and around water. What precautions should parents take to ensure their safety?
2. Why are beach balls, inner tubes, air mattresses and other inflatable devices usually banned from beaches and pools?

3. What is the most dangerous area in a swimming pool? Why?

4. Sunburn is a common problem related to swimming. How can it be prevented and what are the proper first aid procedures to follow for a first degree burn? Second degree burn?

5. Where can you get the training that teaches you how to safely use the aquatic environment for recreational activities?

SELECTED REFERENCES

1. Collis, M. & Kirchoff, B., (1974). *Swimming* . Boston, MA: Allyn and Bacon.

2. Jarvis, M. A., (1972). *Enjoy Swimming.* London, England: Faber and Faber Ltd.

3. Morris, D., (1969). *Swimming.* London, England: Heineman Educational Books.

4. Vickers, B. J., and Vincent, W. J., (1984). *Swimming.* (4th Ed.), Dubuque, Iowa: Wm.C. Brown.

CHAPTER 5

Advice Concerning Irritations, Injuries, and Other Conditions

It is impossible to count the number of times a swimming instructor has heard the question, "Do I have to go in the water today?" This is followed by excuses such as: "I have a cold, or a sore throat, or the flu." Still more disconcerting are the missed classes due to minor skin irritations or injuries. This chapter is designed to discuss common problems that may occur, their effect on participation, and their prevention and care.

SKIN IRRITATIONS AND WOUNDS

Rashes, abrasions and open sores are common problems. The potential for infecting others is an important factor in any decision concerning the feasibility of swimming while affected by one of these skin disorders. The possibility of a wound becoming infected should also be considered.

Rashes

Rashes have either external or internal origins. Externally induced rashes are those which are caused by coming into contact with poisonous plants, bacteria, fungi, or a virus. Examples of rashes caused by an external source would include poison ivy, oak or sumac, impetigo, measles and other communicable diseases. Internally induced rashes are those which are caused by the body's own defense mechanism. Nervousness, the interaction of two or more drugs and food allergies could cause a rash with an internal origin.

Swimming should be avoided when an individual has an externally induced rash which is accompanied by small lesions or a rash that is associated with a fever. In either case, it would be advisable to check with a physician prior to resuming swimming activities.

Since internally induced rashes can not be passed on to others, an individual with this type of rash may continue to participate in swimming. If the symptoms are aggravated by the activity, discontinue swimming and seek the advice of a physician.

Wounds (Abrasions, Cuts and Open Sores)

Open wounds such as large abrasions or deep cuts are subject to infection. Therefore, it is not advisable to participate in aquatic activities until a scab has formed on an abrasion or until a deep cut is closed and dry. Do not participate in swimming activities if the wound becomes infected as evidenced by redness, swelling and the presence of pus. If stitches are required, follow the advice of the physician in terms of re-entering the water.

PREVENTION: It is the responsibility of the swimmer, lifeguard and instructor to make the swimming area a safe place. The swimmer's obedience to the rules will help to prevent accidents such as falling on a slippery deck or hitting one's head on the side of the pool. Supervisory personnel need to keep the area free of all glass and sharp objects. They also need to enforce safety rules.

CARE: If a swimmer gets an abrasion as a result of an accident, the wound should be cleansed and bandaged with a dry, sterile dressing. If a swimmer is cut, elevate the part and hold a hand or a clean cloth tightly over the wound to stop the bleeding. Cleanse the wound with water to remove any sand or debris and bandage firmly with a sterile dressing. A deep or severe cut may continue to bleed profusely. In that case, apply pressure against the brachial artery (if the wound is on the upper extremity) or against the femoral artery (if the wound is on the lower extremity). Call the Emergency Medical Service (EMS), if severe bleeding continues.

EYE, EAR, AND NOSE
IRRITATIONS AND INJURIES

Eye Irritations and Injuries

Eye irritations are one of the most common complaints among those who swim regularly. The cause is often an imbalance in the chemicals used to treat pool water. If either the acidity-alkalinity (ph) level or the chlorine level is too high, the eyes may be effected. The eyes may become red and the vision become "foggy". This condition may last for several hours.

PREVENTION: Prevention may be as simple as purchasing a pair of well-fitting goggles.

CARE: Do not rub the eyes. That will only make them worse. Flush the eyes with tap water and get plenty of rest. The use of a commercial cleansing solution is not recommended because some products may react adversely with the chemicals in the water that caused the problem. If irritation persists, see a physician.

Other Eye Problems

Pink eye is an infection caused by rubbing the eye with germ laden hands. The eye exhibits symptoms of redness, swelling and itching. An ointment can be prescribed by a doctor. After a few days, the swelling will subside. Do not enter the water until the condition has cleared up.

More serious eye irritations and injuries may occur when two people are playing and one person gets poked in the eye, or a person collides with an object in the water. If the eye is bleeding or appears to be severely damaged, bandage both eyes firmly and take the individual to the nearest hospital. Good management of the water facility and good discipline of those who use the facility are tools of prevention.

Earaches

For many, the "joys of summer" include long swims, fun in the sun and acute infections of the outer ear canal. Infections are not really a joy, but the result of long swims or any activity that allows water to enter the ear canal. Moisture in the ear permits bacteria or fungi to infect it. The bacteria are floating in the water or already living in the ear. This painful infection is known as *swimmer's ear*. To detect it, push on the piece of cartilage in front of the ear opening, if there is pain, an infection is present. Ear infections should be treated by a physician. Remain out of the water until the infection is cleared up.

PREVENTION: A commercial preparation called *"Swim Ear"* may be used to help keep the ears dry and free of infection. Doctors suggest that four or five drops of isopropyl alcohol (70 percent) in the ear canal after swimming or showering may dry the ears.

Thoroughly drying the ears with a towel after swimming will also help to prevent infections. Individuals who are prone to ear infections should consider the use of ear plugs prescribed by a specialist.

Nose Irritations

Nose irritations are not as common as those of the eye and ear. However, some pre-adolescents and adults are prone to nosebleeds. They are usually caused by a cold or allergies that inflame the nasal passages. Accidentally bumping the nose or violent nose blowing may also cause a nosebleed. Swimming may be resumed once a nosebleed has been stopped for ten minutes or more.

PREVENTION: Nosebleeds are common in dry climates or during winter months. To prevent them, doctors suggest that a bit of ointment such as petroleum jelly be placed inside the nose at the edge of the nostrils at bedtime.

CARE: It is best to sit down and pinch the nose tightly shut for five to ten minutes. Breathe through the mouth. If bleeding continues, apply a cold pack to the neck and head. Nosebleeds that cannot be stopped within 30 minutes should be considered serious, and the individual should be taken to an emergency facility.

MUSCLE CRAMPS

Muscle cramps have been experienced by swimmers of all ages. They are sudden, sustained, painful contractions of the muscle. They usually occur in a muscle that is tired from intense, prolonged use, and may develop after only a slight contraction. The underlying cause may be an inadequate supply of blood to the tired muscle. Low levels of calcium, sodium or potassium may also precipitate cramps.

Swimmers most often suffer from cramps of the calf, foot or toes. These are frequently the result of vigorous kicking during the crawl stroke. Although muscle cramps are painful, they usually last only a short time. Once a cramp has been relieved, the swimmer should use another stroke to continue swimming.

PREVENTION: Stretching exercises prior to entering the water may help to prevent the onset of cramps. Muscle cramps caused by inadequate levels of calcium, sodium or potassium can be avoided through dietary supplementation.

CARE: Cramps can be relieved by applying firm pressure to massage the affected muscle along with stretching it. The muscle of the calf can be stretched by pulling the foot toward the shin while the knee is extended. The muscles of the foot can also be stretched by pulling the foot up towards the front of the shin.

INFECTIONS OF THE FEET

Athlete's Foot

Athlete's foot is caused by the fungi, *tinea pedis*, which is prevalent in locker rooms and shower rooms. A case of athlete's foot is accompanied by an itchy, burning feeling. Small blisters and peeling skin are found between the toes. There is no need to discontinue swimming during an outbreak of athlete's foot.

PREVENTION: Dry the feet thoroughly after swimming or showering; especially the area between the toes. Wear one hundred percent cotton socks to absorb perspiration and keep the feet dry. Change socks frequently.

CARE: Once infected with athlete's foot fungi, treat as follows: 1. Dry the feet thoroughly after swimming or showering. 2. Apply an over-the-counter antifungal ointment or spray to the affected area twice daily. 3. Use an antifungal powder to help keep the feet dry.

Plantar's Warts

Plantar's warts are caused by a virus that invades the skin, usually through a cut or abrasion in the bottom of the foot. Tiny black dots (blood vessels) form on the surface and nourish the wart. These warts may become large and quite painful. There is no need to refrain from swimming because of warts. They should, however, be treated.

CARE: Some warts disappear without any treatment. A commercial acid solution may be used to irritate the wart and cause it to go into remission. Since serious complications may result, diabetics and those with poor blood circulation should seek medical care rather than using a commercial preparation. If the wart hurts and causes limping, see a podiatrist.

VIRAL INFECTIONS

Colds and Fever

Contrary to popular belief, swimming does not increase susceptibility to colds and throat infections. A "cold" is the name given to over 200 relatively minor viral infections that are transmitted primarily through hand contact. Covering the mouth with the hand for a sneeze or a cough is a thoughtful effort. However, if the hand is then extended to others, the "germs" will be passed to them.

There is a greater chance of catching a cold in a warm, dry, crowded classroom than in a swimming pool in the middle of the winter. Research indicates that students who swim often during the winter miss less school due to colds and respiratory infections than non-swimming students.

Swimming while affected with a minor cold will not cause it to become worse. If a fever accompanies the cold, refrain from swimming.

PREVENTION: Frequent hand washing is the best protection against cold viruses. Proper eating and sleeping habits may also help to reduce the incidence of colds.

CARE: Cold symptoms such as a stuffy or runny nose; sneezing; watery, itchy eyes; minor aches and pains; or a sinus headache can usually be helped by over-the-counter cold remedies. If the cold becomes worse and a high fever develops, see a doctor.

Throat Infections

A sore throat frequently accompanies a cold. Often it is one of the first signs that a cold is coming. It may be caused by either a viral or a bacterial infection. In the event of any throat infection, do not swim.

CARE: Gargling with salt water (one-half teaspoon of salt in a glass of warm water) may help to relieve throat pain as well as help in the healing process. Over-the-counter (OTC) throat lozenges or sprays such as those containing benzocaine may reduce the soreness and pain. Drink plenty of liquids, swallow frequently and increase the humidity of the environment.

Strep throat is a serious, contagious inflammation of the throat that may accompany a cold. A doctor must do a throat culture to establish the cause of the inflammation. If it is caused by a virus, it will usually disappear within three to five days. If it is caused by bacteria, antibiotics must be used and it will linger from one to two weeks.

SHOULDER AND KNEE DISCOMFORT

Tendonitis of the Shoulder

Inflammation of the shoulder caused by the rubbing of ligaments and tendons against the boney parts of the joints is referred to as tendonitis. In swimming it may result from overuse of the shoulder joint as the crawl stroke is repeated over great distances in practice.

PREVENTION: A proper warm-up which includes stretching prior to engaging in lap swimming may help to prevent or alleviate tendonitis.

CARE: The first step in the care of tendonitis is to ice the painful area. If pain persists, shorten the workout or change the strokes used. If relief is not obtained, see a physician.

Knee Joint Injuries

Most knee joint pain that occurs in swimming is associated with the whip kick. An individual who has suffered a previous knee injury may experience pain while executing the whip kick. Those with no previous history of knee problems could also develop pain in the knee joint. This may be the result of overuse caused by repeated attempts to perform the whip kick. In either case, the individual may experience inflammation of the knee joint.

Whether or not an individual continues to swim while recuperating is up to the individual and his physician. In any case, the swimmer should use a kick that does not place further stress on the knee.

PREVENTION: It may be possible to eliminate or alleviate chronic knee pain associated with the whip kick. This can be done by slightly increasing the distance between the knees during the kick. Warm-up exercises may also be beneficial.

CARE: Apply cold, wet packs or a small bag of ice to the affected area. A reduction in the amount of activity and/or resting the joint will promote healing. If pain persists, seek the advice of a physician.

WOMEN'S CONCERNS

Menstruation

A common misconception, even today, is that swimming during the menstrual period may be harmful. This is simply not true. The phase of the monthly cycle has little effect on either the ability to participate in or perform physical activities. In fact, Olympic gold medals have been won by women swimmers and others during all phases of the monthly cycle.

Young girls and women can look forward to continuing to participate in swimming activities during their periods. The use of a tampon will give them the protection that they need. The cold water may even slow down the menstrual flow or stop it temporarily.

Pregnancy

Another misconception relates to swimming during pregnancy. In the past, some women have considered swimming during the third trimester of pregnancy to be harmful. This is not true. Swimming is actually one of the safest physical activities for women at all stages of pregnancy.

The buoyant effect of the water helps to relieve back pain that is prevalent during the latter stages of pregnancy. The water also prevents the jarring of the body that often occurs in land sport activities.

Strokes done in a prone (front lying) position or side lying position are most comfortable late in pregnancy. These include the breast stroke, sidestroke, and a modified front crawl stroke. Excessive kicking is tiresome and not recommended. Water exercise classes are excellent for the mother-to-be.

Research indicates that women who exercise during pregnancy have a shorter labor and an easier delivery. It is also reported that maintaining good muscle tone and cardiovascular fitness during pregnancy reduces figure restoration time. One swimming instructor reported that she taught classes until late in January, had the baby the first week of February, and was back teaching and coaching the next week. She experienced restoration of her figure within one month.

Pregnant women should exercise caution in the pool area. They should walk slower than normal on wet surfaces. They should rest frequently and avoid becoming excessively tired. Chilling should be avoided by keeping a large towel or sweatsuit near the water's edge.

Enjoyment of the water and swimming activities need not be denied to women because of menstruation or pregnancy. Proper care of the body, will allow for full participation in aquatic activities at all times.

SUMMARY

In this chapter, an attempt was made to identify some physical problems that may or may not affect participation. Each problem that was identified was discussed in terms of its cause, prevention and care. In many instances, the feasibility of continuing swimming through the identified difficulty was discussed. It must be understood that the severity of a given situation may affect the ability of the individual to participate. When in doubt, seek the advice of a physician.

REVIEW QUESTIONS

1. Under what conditions should swimming with a rash be avoided?
2. What can be done for the individual who suffers tendonitis of the shoulder joint?
3. Will swimming in extremely cold weather cause a cold? Explain.
4. Discuss the following statement: Pregnant women should stay out of the water to avoid harm to the baby.
5. How can muscle cramps be relieved?

SELECTED REFERENCES

1. Aaron, J. E., Bridges, A. F., & Ritzel D. O., (1972). *First Aid and Emergency Care.* New York, NY: Macmillan.
2. American National Red Cross. (1981). *Standard First Aid and Personal Safety.* Washington, DC: American Red Cross.
3. Maglischo, E. W., & Brennan, C. F., (1985). *Swim for the Health of It.* Palo Alto, CA: Mayfield.
4. Michaud, E. & Anastas, L. L., (1988). *Listen to Your Body.* Emmaus, PA: Rodale.

CHAPTER 6
Water Adjustment Skills

Man was designed to experience life in an upright position using his lower limbs to walk or run on solid ground. His breathing mechanism was designed to extract oxygen directly from the air. When he is first exposed to a water environment, his movements are awkward and inefficient and he experiences difficulty in breathing. With proper acclimation to the water and training, he can develop skills that will greatly enhance his ability to move in the water.

This chapter contains many self help skills for the non-swimmer. Read the instructions carefully and practice the skills in the water. Each of the skills in this chapter should be mastered before proceeding to learn the basic strokes as discussed in the next chapter.

IMMERSION OF THE BODY

For the individual without any prior experience in a body of water, the thought of going under water can create very real fears. Knowledge is a key factor in helping the novice swimmer overcome his fears. (See Appendix C).

Temperature, pressure, and buoyancy are three elements that affect a body which is immersed in water. A knowledge of the effects of each of these elements will be beneficial to the novice as he becomes acclimated to the water.

The first hurdle the student faces is adjusting to the water temperature. Bath water is usually ninety degrees or hotter. Lake and pool temperatures vary, but they are usually considerably colder. Entering water as cool as eighty degrees will cause elevation of respiratory and pulse rates. The body may also react with a slight shiver upon entering the water. This indicates that the body is attempting to conserve its heat, which may even cause "goose bumps" to appear.

Gradually entering the pool or lake will help in the acclimation process. At a lake, step in, walk to knee high level and begin to gather water in the hands and wet down the arms and upper legs. Then splash a little water on the chest, neck, and face. At a pool this process can begin while sitting on the edge with the legs in the water.

Water acclimation may be further enhanced by trying the following activities.

1. In a lake or shallow pool, sit in the shallow water and place the arms behind the hips with the hands on the bottom. Lean back until the ears are at water level.

2. In the same position, balance the body on the hands and let the legs rise to the top of the water. Turn over, place the hands on the bottom and move the body backwards and forwards by walking on the hands letting the legs float upwards.

3. Walking, running or skipping in shallow water are also good ways to become accustomed to being in the water.

Water pressure will be felt when the student enters chest deep water. The student may experience a slight increase in difficulty of breathing. Although the novice swimmer will experience some pressure upon total body immersion, he will not feel a great deal of water pressure until he is able to swim under water and dive down eight to ten feet. At that time the student will experience pressure in the ears. Pressure will increase at greater depths, and is usually relieved by swallowing.

BUOYANCY

Most individuals will be pleasantly surprised to discover that the water exerts an upward force on the body which supports it at or near the surface. This upward force is called buoyancy. Buoyancy is such a strong force that scuba divers must wear belts with lead weights in order to sink toward the bottom. The buoyant force of the water is a benefit to the disabled since it increases the ability to move in the water.

Buoyancy varies greatly from one individual to the next. One individual will float in a horizontal position at the surface of the water. Another may float with his legs dropped to a 45 degree angle from the surface. A third may float in a vertical position. There are also a few individuals who find that they cannot float, but must keep moving to remain on the surface.

The position in which one floats is determined by the individual's body composition. An individual with a large amount of adipose (fatty) tissue will float in a horizontal position. This is because the density of adipose tissue is less than the density of the water. Therefore, the water is able to exert a greater upward force in relation to the downward force of the body. At the other extreme, is the individual who is heavily muscled and has very little subcutaneous fat. The muscular body is very dense because there is so little adipose tissue in relation to the amount of muscle tissue and bone. The density of the body is greater than the density of the water. Therefore, the person will tend to sink.

Fortunately, most individuals lie somewhere between these two extremes. Women have a larger percentage of adipose tissue than men, and have a tendency to float in a near horizontal position. Men, on the other hand, usually have a greater percentage of lean body mass (muscle and bone). As a group, they tend to float more toward a vertical position.

SUBMERSION OF THE BODY AND FACE

Submersion of the entire body under water is a giant step beyond immersion of the body to shoulder level, particularly for adults. The older novice swimmer has more fear which makes it more difficult to put one's face in cold water.

Fears related to water and learning which have accumulated over the years can be alleviated through knowledge and experience. Several activities are listed below which can be used to gain skill and confidence in a non-swimming setting.

1. While showering, the water usually runs down the face. Tub lovers should try the shower experience, and wash their hair in the shower. Try to open the eyes while the warm water runs down the hair and face during the rinse cycle.

2. Fill the sink full of tepid water, place the face in the water. Begin to blow bubbles, continue for as long as possible. Try to open the eyes and see the bubbles that are created.

3. Try putting your face in the pool water and looking to see where colored diving rings are located, or to count the number of fingers a partner has revealed under the water.

When body immersion and total body submersion have been mastered, the student is ready to learn the floating skills.

BOBBING, BREATH CONTROL

Bobbing is a skill which is used to teach the beginning swimmer how to control the breathing process. The beginner should stand in shoulder deep water (holding on to the side of the pool) and begin to submerge the entire body by bending the knees. Take a deep breath before submerging. Blow out bubbles through the mouth and nose as the face enters the water. Continue blowing until the head comes back up out of the water. Submerge only as far as the eyebrows, which is the depth needed for most swimming strokes. To recover, quickly extend the knees and return to a standing position. As the mouth emerges from the water, inhale in preparation to submerge again. Repeat this action continuously eight to ten times. After a few tries, open the eyes while under water. Vision may be blurred at first, but seeing underwater is an important safety skill. When the water chemistry is not properly balanced, the eyes may burn. In that case, a pair of well-fitting goggles are recommended.

RHYTHMIC BREATHING

Breath control involves rhythmic breathing. Rhythmic breathing means inhaling air with the face out of the water and exhaling air into the water in a continuous pattern similar to breathing when out of the water. Those who have had a First Aid class know that a person normally breathes 12 times a minute, or once every five seconds. Beginners tend to breath at a faster rate in water because of fears related to submersion of the face and drowning. Normal breathing in water is estimated to be 12 to 18 times per minute.

There are several methods used to practice rhythmic breathing. One is to stand at the side of the pool in waist to chest deep water, holding on to the side of the pool with one hand. Place the head horizontally on its side in the water so that the water covers the ear and comes up to the lower corner of the mouth. Take a quick breath, inhaling through the mouth. Rotate the head to a face down position. The head should be immersed to a point that the water meets the hairline. Completely exhale through the mouth and nose. Rotate the head to the starting position and inhale. Repeat this process once every four or five seconds for approximately one minute.

For more practice, have a partner count the number of times breathing occurs during a two minute time period. Divide the number of breaths by two to see if it falls within the suggested range of 12 to 18 times per minute. Repeat the practice with the necessary adjustments until breathing rhythmically in the water feels comfortable.

Another method used to practice rhythmic breathing is through the use of various games. The Ostrich game is played by putting the face down in the water (as the ostrich does in the sand). To determine if the game warden is near, he turns his face to the side, takes in air, turns back, and exhales. A person is caught when tapped as he comes up for air. Other tag games can be invented that use rhythmic breathing.

FLOATING

There are three types of floats: the jellyfish, prone and back float. Master each before proceeding to the other swimming skills.

Jellyfish Float

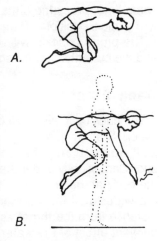

The jellyfish float is also called the tuck float. It can be performed in waist deep water. Reach down and place both hands at the knees. Take a deep breath, placing the face in the water. Grasp both knees and bring them to the chest, let the back bob to the top of the water as the breath is held. Hold for a few moments. Let go of the knees, extend the legs toward the bottom and lift the head while pushing the arms down and backwards until the body is upright.

This float is the basic position to use in learning survival skills, and the tuck surface dive. It also serves to further acquaint the student with the buoyant effect of the water.

A. Jellyfish float position
B. Recovery from jellyfish float

Prone Float

The prone float, also called the front or "Dead Man's" float, can be performed in water two to three feet deep. Kneel down in the water, place the hands on the bottom, keeping the head up. Extend the legs backward, take a deep breath, place the face in the water to ear level. Slowly let the hands and arms rise to the top of the water. Hold the body as straight as possible for a few moments. Recover by lifting the head and bending the hips, letting the knees contact the bottom. At the same time, press the arms and hands down until they come in contact with the bottom.

A.

A. Prone float   B. Recovery from prone float

B.

To begin the prone float in deeper water, stand with one foot eight to ten inches in front of the other foot. Bend the knees to lower the body to a point where the shoulders are in the water. Extend both arms out in front of the body at the surface of the water. Take a deep breath, place the face in the water and use the legs to push the body forward. Allow the feet to rise to the surface. To recover to a standing position, lift the head and bend the hips as the knees are drawn to the chest. At the same time, press the arms and hands down and back to rotate the body to a vertical position. Then extend the legs toward the bottom surface.

The prone position will be used in the crawl stroke, the breaststroke, and the butterfly. It will also be used to begin the pike surface dive.

Back Float

The back float, also called the supine float, can be learned in waist deep water. Start by assuming a high kneeling position in the water with the hip joint straight and the back slightly arched. This should place the shoulders slightly under the water. Extend the arms out from the sides of the body at the surface of the water for balance. Rest the head back in the water until the ears are barely covered. Keep the chin the same distance from the throat as if you were standing. Lean back and let the buoyant effect of the water begin to lift the body. Keep the back arched as the body rises and hold for a few seconds. This is a back float. To recover to a standing position, pull the head forward, bend the hips and sweep the arms back and down and then forward.

Once this simple technique has been experienced, the novice is ready to attempt the back float from a standing position. Start with the feet spread in a forward/backward stride. Bend the knees so that the shoulders are submerged. Tilt the head back, extend the arms out from the sides of the body and use the feet to gently push off in a backward direction. This will put the body into a back floating position. It is very important that the back remains arched with the hips at or near the surface of the water. Maintain that position in the water for a short time before trying to regain a standing position. To stand, lift the head, bend at the hips pulling the knees toward the chest, and sweep the arms back and down and then forward. When the body is in an upright position, extend the legs so that they touch the bottom.

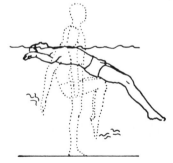

Back float and recovery from back float

Many people find that they do not float in a horizontal position. They are suspended somewhere between a horizontal and a vertical position. This is normal. There are, however, several things that can be done to bring the body closer to a horizontal position. These include:

✔ Moving the arms in the water to a position above the head.

✔ With the arms in the overhead position, flex the wrists to cause the fingers to point up out of the water.

✔ Adjust the breathing so that the lungs are fully inflated most of the time. To do this, it is necessary to take a deep breath, hold it, exhale forcefully, and then inhale quickly.

✔ Flex the knees to bring the feet under the buttocks while keeping the hips extended and the back slightly arched.

The back float is the basic body position to assume before beginning to swim the elementary backstroke, the back crawl, and the inverted breaststroke.

GLIDING

There are two basic glides and kick glides. They are performed in the prone and back float positions.

Prone Glide

The prone glide is actually a prone float in which the body is propelled forward through the water. Propulsion is achieved by exerting a backward push with the feet against the pool bottom.

To perform the prone glide, start in about four feet of water with the feet spread 10 to 12 inches apart in a forward/backward stride position. Bend the knees to bring the shoulders just below the surface of the water. Place the hands together with the arms extended in front of the body at the surface of the water. Lean forward, place the face in the water and push back against the bottom with the feet. Push hard enough to travel across the water a distance of at least two body lengths.

When properly performed, the face should be in the water with the arms extended close together out in front of the body and the legs straight with the toes pointed. Thus the body is streamlined as it moves through the water. When forward momentum ceases, recover to a standing position using the same technique as in the prone float.

Back Glide

The back glide is a back float with propulsive force which causes the body to move backward through the water. It is performed by assuming the back float starting position, with the arms at the sides. Bend the knees to submerge the shoulders in the water. Tilt the head back so that the ears are in the water and push with the feet. Keep the legs together and the arms at the sides to maintain a streamlined position. When momentum is lost, use the techniques discussed above under back float to recover to a standing position.

Before beginning the backward thrust of the legs, look to be sure that the space is clear. This will help to eliminate the possibility of an accident. Push only hard enough to send the body backwards six to eight feet.

KICK GLIDES

The prone and back kick glides combine the action of the float, the glide, and the flutter kick.

Prone Kick Glide

Start by pushing off into a prone glide, then begin kicking alternately with the legs. This leg action is commonly called the flutter kick. It is used in the front and back crawl strokes.

The flutter kick involves an alternate up and down movement of the legs, with one leg in an up position, while the other is in a down position. The action begins at the hip. As the leg presses down, water pressure will cause a slight natural bend to the knee. As the leg moves up toward the surface, water pressure will tend to straighten the knee. The knees should remain "relaxed" throughout the kicking movement with emphasis on the upward phase of the kick. The ankles should also remain relaxed so that the feet can act as flippers pushing up and down in the water. Turn the toes in to create a slightly pigeon-toe effect. Kick no deeper than 14 to 16 inches and allow the heels to just barley break the surface of the water, resulting in a maximum of a six inch spray.

Back Kick Glide

The back kick glide begins with a back glide. Once the body has begun to move, begin the alternate leg action of the flutter kick. Kick from the hip with an extended knee as the leg moves downward into the water. The upward phase of the kick should be emphasized. As the lifting action begins at the hip, the knee is in a bent position. As the upward movement continues, the leg is forcefully straightened causing large amounts of water to be forced to the surface. Keep the ankles extended throughout the kick. Use a deep, rapid kick in which the feet do not break the surface of the water.

JUMPING IN WATER, LEVELING OFF

As a preliminary step to jumping into deep water, the beginner should practice jumping into shallow water (three to four feet deep). Even though the face will probably not submerge, there will be water splashed in the face. To some beginners, this poses a threat. To help to alleviate such fears, water acclimation and adjustment must be accomplished prior to attempting to jump.

When jumping, the beginner should absorb the force of landing on the bottom of the pool by bending the hips, knees and ankles at the moment of impact, to absorb the force of the landing. This action will also lower the body in the water. Once the beginner has landed, he should extend his arms in front of his body at the surface of the water. He should take a deep breath, place the head in the water and push off into a prone glide position. The student should continue practicing this skill in shallow water until he becomes thoroughly familiar with it. For variety, he can push off into a prone glide, roll to the supine position and then back to the prone position.

Once the beginner has mastered jumping into shallow water, he can move to deeper water. It would be a good idea to move to water that is only slightly over the head at this time. Practice jumping, landing with the knees, hips and ankles flexed, and pushing off diagonally forward and upward into a horizontal position at the surface. The beginner should begin exhaling through the mouth and nose before he enters the water. This will prevent water from being forced up the nostrils as the head submerges.

The beginner who has become comfortable jumping into water that is slightly over his head, should be ready to jump into water that is ten feet deep or more. By jumping with the feet spread, the arms away from his sides and a slight forward lean to the trunk, he can slow his descent. He will probably not touch the bottom. He can easily return to the surface by forcefully bringing the arms and legs together. By leaning the trunk forward with the head down, he will be able to gain a horizontal position at the surface as he moves his arms in a downward and backward direction while kicking the legs. Once at the surface, the beginner should begin to move through the water in a prone position or roll over onto the back.

ADAPTATIONS FOR THE DISABLED

Generally, immersion in the water is as fearful for the disabled beginner as it is for other beginning swimmers. The mental and physical adjustment entails having a positive attitude toward learning to move and swim in the water, and getting in and trying one's best. Flotation devices can assist until independent mobility is achieved. Warmer than normal water (85 degrees) is more conducive to staying in the water for a 30 minute swim lesson.

Personal adaptations for staying afloat, gliding, and kicking may have to be made according to the specific disability. Much practice will be needed for achieving the desired result. Patience is a necessity for the student and instructor alike. Ask the instructor for an aide to help in class or have a friend who is a swimmer assist you in the class. If learning to swim is important, don't become discouraged. Keep working at the water adjustment skills, then the swimming strokes will be easier to learn.

SUMMARY

Water adjustment activities are designed to help the student become accustomed to the water and its effects on the body. A student who has had no previous experience in swimming should take the time to become thoroughly familiar with the water and experience its buoyant effects. Practice and master each skill described in this chapter. Then the student will be ready to be challenged by the skills covered in the next four chapters.

REVIEW QUESTIONS

1. Why do men have more difficulty floating then women do?
2. What are three things that can be done to help a person float in a better position?
3. Discuss methods of becoming acclimated to the water.
4. What must be done to come to a standing position from a prone float position?
5. List three types of floats.

SELECTED REFERENCES

1. American National Red Cross. (1977). *Adapted Aquatics*. Washington, DC: American National Red Cross.
2. American National Red Cross. (1981). *Manual for the Basic Swimming Instructor*. Washington, DC: American National Red Cross.
3. Harris, M. M., (1969). *Basic Swimming Analyzed*. Boston, MA: Allyn and Bacon.
4. Jarvis, M. A., (1972). *Enjoy Swimming*. London: Faber and Faber, Ltd.
5. Mackenzie, M. M. & Spears, B., (1982). *Beginning Swimming*. Belmont, CA: Wadsworth.
6. Vickers, B. J. & Vincent, W. J., (1984). *Swimming*. (4th Ed.) Dubuque, IA: Wm. C. Brown.

CHAPTER 7
Basic Swimming Strokes

Movement on land differs greatly from movement in water due to the properties of water and the laws of movement in water. Running on land is not greatly affected by air density or temperature. However, running in water such as in water exercise, is greatly impeded by the density and buoyancy of the water. Movement on land is usually in an upright or vertical position, body movement in water is most often in a horizontal position.

APPLICATION OF
PHYSICAL LAWS TO SWIMMING

A swimmer's forward speed is the result of two forces, resistance and propulsion. Resistance is a force that retards movement through the water. The force that pushes the body forward is called propulsion. It is created by arm and leg movements. In order to swim faster, a swimmer must decrease the resistance force and increase the propulsive force. For example, assuming a horizontal position and decreasing the depth of the kick in a crawl stroke creates less resistance and increases propulsion.

Types of Resistance

Three types of water resistance have been identified. They are: *form drag*, *wave drag* and *body surface drag*.

Form drag is the resistance created by the outline or shape of the body and its parts as it moves through the water. A high pressure area is created along the leading edge of the body since it must "break through the water" to create a path for the body to move through. A low pressure area is created behind the body which results in turbulence or eddies. The suction created by the turbulence produces a force in opposition to the movement of the body. This decreases the speed of the swimmer.

A breaststroker who flexes the hips and knees excessively during the recovery phase of the kick would have increased form drag. Since the body is not streamlined, greater turbulence would develop behind the feet. Form drag is also increased when the swimmer raises the head so that the body and legs drop in the water.

Wave drag is a type of resistance caused by the waves created by the body as it moves through the water. The waves produce a force which is in opposition to the direction of body movement. Wave drag is directly proportional to swimming speed. In other words, as speed increases wave drag increases. Wave drag is increased as the head rises to breathe in the breaststroke, since this action magnifies the size of the wave in front of the shoulders. Wave drag is beneficial to the freestyler since it creates a bow wave known as a "pocket of air" which allows the swimmer to breathe with a minimal amount of head rotation.

Body surface drag is the resistance caused by the condition of the surface of the body as it moves through the water. Body surface drag can be reduced by wearing a swimming cap, by removing body hair and by selecting a tight fitting, sleek swimsuit. For a woman, a one or two piece suit with ruffles or a blousey top would create more water resistance than a skin tight one piece suit.

Men's competitive style swimming suits create considerably less body surface drag than women's suits. Greasing down the body with a slippery substance would decrease body surface drag. Although decreasing water resistance by streamlining the body position would be helpful to all swimmers; hair, shaving and body greasing would not be appropriate for the recreational swimmer.

Newton's Laws of Motion

Force must be applied by the body to move it, keep it in motion or change its direction. This principle is known as the Law of Inertia or *Newton's First Law of Motion*. Examples of the application of this law in swimming would include:

1. After the push-off for a turn, the body slows down as it glides through the water. In order to keep the body in motion, a force must be applied through the use of arm and/or leg movements.

2. To turn around and swim back to the side of the pool the swimmer must exert a force against the water in a diagonal direction rather then directly backward as one would do to go straight ahead.

3. If a swimmer floated motionless on the surface of the water, his body would not move unless a force was exerted. The force could be wave action or the movement of the limbs.

Newton's second law, the *Law of Acceleration* states that the speed of the body is in direct proportion to the amount of force applied. In swimming the force is applied by the use of the arms and the legs. If a swimmer is able to increase the amount of force that is applied against the water, his speed will increase. An example of this law can be seen by looking at the arm action in the front crawl. If a swimmer keeps the elbow high during the force phase of the arm stroke, much more force is created against the water then if the elbow is dropped during the early part of the pull. All other things being equal, the swimmer will increase his speed.

Newton's third law, the *Law of Reaction*, states that for every action there is an equal and opposite reaction. In swimming, the action is the water being forced backward by the arms and legs, and the reaction is the movement of the body in a forward direction. Since the reaction will be in a direction directly opposite that of the action, it is important that the swimmer push the water straight backwards rather then up, down, or to the side. An arm pattern that forces water in any other direction will result in changing the path of the body through the water.

STROKE RHYTHM AND COMFORT

Each stroke has its own rhythm which is related to the particular type of kick and arm pattern used as well as the established timing of the arms, legs and breathing. Some strokes such as the elementary backstroke have a pause or glide which serves as a break in the rhythm. Other strokes such as the front crawl have a continuous action in which the arms and legs are moving at different speeds. This is due to the different distances that they travel during a stroke cycle.

Development of good stroke rhythm is dependent upon the swimmer's ability to tense and relax muscles as needed throughout the movement. As a swimmer improves in skill, body movements will become less rigid and more fluid. This will not only improve one's rhythmic pattern, but it will enhance the ability to comfortably swim for distance.

Successful performance of swimming strokes depends upon a person's familiarity with the water and his ability to float comfortably. All strokes begin with good body position in the water. The body should be stretched out and level in the water with the head, hips, and heels high. The stroke will be performed either in a face down (prone) position as in the crawl or breaststroke, or in a face up (supine) position as in the back strokes. In the prone position strokes, it is necessary to learn rhythmic breathing before attempting to learn the mechanics of the stroke.

ELEMENTARY BACKSTROKE

The elementary backstroke is one of the first strokes a beginner learns. Regular breathing is encouraged since the face is out of the water in this stroke. Since a good elementary backstroke is very relaxed, it can be used to travel long distances in comfort.

Starting Body Position

The starting body position is on the back with both arms and hands at the side of the body, and the fingers touching the thighs. The head is slightly out of the water (ear level). The hips are slightly below the water level with the legs together and no more than six to eight inches deep. The starting position is identical to the ending position in which the swimmer glides.

Arm Motion

The arm motion begins by recovery to a position which will allow force to be applied. With the arms held to the sides and the palms against the thighs, begin to draw the hands up the sides of the body, thumbs leading. Keep the elbows down to decrease water resistance. Turn the hands outward when they reach armpit level. Extend both arms sideward with the palms of the hands facing the feet. The arms should be extended approximately eight to ten inches above shoulder level. Pause slightly.

The force phase immediately follows the momentary pause. With the arms straight or slightly bent and just below the surface of the water, push water toward the feet. The fingers should be slightly spread and relaxed. Be sure that the hands remain underwater throughout the stroke. The palms of the hands should finish against the thighs. The arm pull provides the majority of force to move the body through the water and make progress in this stroke.

Whip Kick (Supine)

The kick begins by recovering in preparation for exerting force backwards against the water. From the basic body position with the feet together, both lower legs are dropped into the water by bending the knees to a 90 degree angle. The hip joint must remain extended in order to prevent the knees from coming out of the water. The knees spread slightly so that the kneecaps are lined up with the hip joints. For an adult this would be approximately ten to twelve inches apart or slightly wider than the hips. The toes point upward and outward and the heels are

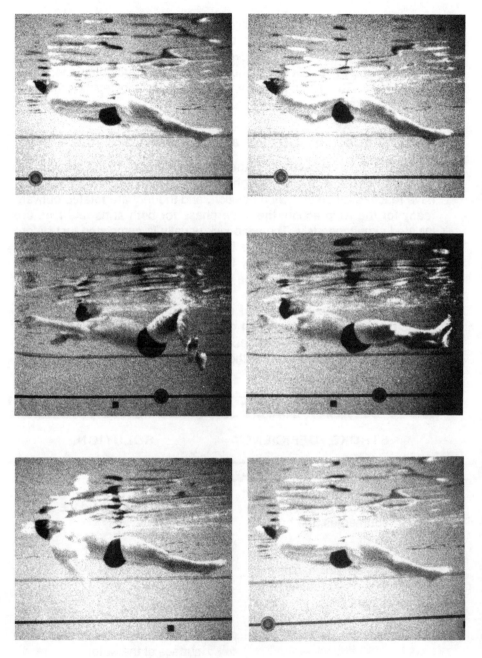

The Elementary Backstroke

drawn apart to a position directly below the knees. The force phase begins by squeezing the inside of the lower legs together. The legs move forcefully around and up toward the top of the water just as in the snap of a whip. The kick ends when both legs are straight and together, toes pointed. The action is similar to using a soccer instep kick with both legs at the same time.

Coordination of Stroke and Breathing Cycle

After the arms have come up the sides of the body to the armpits, the lower part of the legs drop straight down in the water. When the arms have reached an outstretched position, and the feet are rotated outward ready for the whip action, the force phase for both arms and legs are initiated simultaneously. The whip kick usually is completed just before the arms reach the sides of the body. The stroke ends with the legs straight and together. The body is thrust through the water in what is called a "glide." At the end of the glide, the recovery phases of the arm and leg action are again initiated.

The breathing action is not of great importance for the elementary backstroke since the face is out of the water during all phases of the stroke. It is commonly suggested that a person inhale during the recovery phase and exhale during the force phase.

Troubleshooting the Elementary Backstroke

STROKE DEFICIENCY	SOLUTION
Body Position	
If head is back, the face submerges, the back arches.	Drop the chin toward the chest.
If head is high, hips and legs drop creating resistance.	Lower head in the water to ear level.
Sitting in the water.	Raise the hips toward the surface of the water.

Arm Stroke

In recovery, arms begin to extend at chest level.	Bring hands up to armpits before extending arms.
Recover in front of chest causing water to splash face.	Keep thumbs touching body all the way to armpits.
Lift hands or arms out of water.	Keep hands underwater during extension and push.
Reach too far above head during extension.	Extend arms out no more than 8 to 10" above the shoulders.
Stop pull before arms reach thighs, arms drift.	Press back against water all the way to the thigh.

Leg Kick

Knees above water during recovery.	Straighten hips and back, check body position.
Knees outside of feet before thrust causing a frog kick.	Keep knees straight in line with hips, 10"-12" apart. Heels move to a position wider than the knees.
Scissors kick.	Keep body flat on surface. Keep leg movements symmetrical with ankles flexed.
Kicking too fast.	Make thrust strong and full.
Keeping knees together for kick.	Widen knees to hip width before whip action.

Coordination

Leg recovery starts before arms.	Keep legs straight until hands are at armpits.
Sit during recovery.	Press the hips toward the surface throughout.
Glide too short or too long.	Glide until the momentum decreases, then begin next stroke.
Feet drift at end of glide.	Finish kick with ankles and legs together, hold during glide.

SIDESTROKE

The sidestroke is frequently the second of the basic strokes taught to college students because it is one of the easier strokes to learn. The face is out of the water in this stroke. Therefore, the novice swimmer is less apprehensive and does not need to be concerned about difficulties that may arise in learning rhythmic breathing. The sidestroke is not a competitive stroke. It is a resting stroke which is used by many individuals for long distance swimming. It is also useful in lifeguarding to bring a victim to shore. The scissors kick is inverted with the top leg going backward so as not to kick the victim who is being rescued.

Starting Body Position

The body is lying on its side in the water with the bottom arm extended overhead in line with the body. The legs are extended and together. The top arm is resting with the palm down on top of the thigh.

The head should be lying on its side in the water up to the corner of the mouth. The swimmer should look forward or slightly downward. For long distance swims, it is most comfortable to rest the head on the shoulder of the extended bottom arm.

Arm Motion

The arms work alternately. As one arm exerts force, the other arm recovers until the glide when they both rest momentarily.

Bottom Arm

During the first phase of the stroke, force is exerted by the bottom arm. This is accomplished by pressing the arm down approximately twelve inches into the water. Then begin bending the elbow as the arm continues to press. At this point water will be pushed back toward the feet by the hand and forearm. Finish the pull with the elbow directly under the shoulder.

The second phase or recovery phase begins with the elbow under the shoulder. Tuck the elbow tightly to the side with the palm of the hand facing up and under the ear. Extend the arm up past the head and turn the palm of the hand over.

The bottom arm motion concludes with a glide. It remains in the extended position attained at the end of the recovery phase.

Top Arm

The top arm begins by recovering to a position in which it can exert force against the water. It starts with the elbow straight and the palm facing down and resting on the thigh. The hand is drawn across the abdomen and up to the opposite shoulder. The hand is kept close to the body. The palm is rotated toward the feet at the end of the recovery phase.

Begin the force phase by using the palm and forearm to press water toward the feet. Keep the hand within two inches of the body as the press is continued. Finish with the elbow extended, and the hand on top of the thigh.

Scissors Kick

The kick used in the sidestroke is called a scissors kick because of its resemblance to a large scissors cutting through the water. The starting position is with both legs fully extended and with the feet together.

The recovery phase is executed with as little effort as possible. Draw both heels up toward the buttocks, with the knees held close together. The hips should be slightly flexed. The top of the feet should be drawn toward the shin. At this point, the legs begin to separate in a forward-backward direction. The thigh of the top leg (leg nearest the surface) moves forward and upward while the knee joint remains flexed. The bottom leg extends backward at the same time. It stretches as far back as possible to prepare for the thrust or force phase.

The force phase begins with the top leg extending forward at the same time the bottom leg reaches backwards (as a pair of open scissors). When fully extended, the legs squeeze downward and together forcefully thrusting the body forward. The force phase ends when both legs are together, ankles are on top of one another and the toes are pointed.

The kick finishes with a glide (the portion of the kick in which the starting position is held). When body momentum slows down, the stroke begins again.

Coordination of Stroke and Breathing Cycle

The coordination of the sidestroke can be explained in three stages. In the first stage the bottom arm is in the force phase of the stroke while the top arm and legs are in the recovery phase. The bottom arm presses downward and backward against the water as the top arm draws across the abdomen and up to the opposite shoulder. At the same time both legs are drawn up and separated in preparation for the force phase.

The Sidestroke

At the beginning of the second stage of the stroke the bottom arm recovers to its starting position as the top arm and both legs exert force against the water. The bottom arm extends past the head while the top arm pushes water toward the feet as it returns to its position along the thigh. At the same time, the legs are squeezed together.

The third stage of the sidestroke is the glide. In this stage the body is stretched out, with the bottom arm extended above the head, the legs together and the toes pointed. In this streamlined position, the body moves forward some distance without using any arm or leg action. When momentum decreases, a new stroke cycle is begun.

The timing of the breathing sequence does not need to be a real concern since the face is out of the water. Take a breath whenever it is comfortable, but breathe as normally as possible.

TROUBLESHOOTING THE SIDESTROKE

STROKE DEFICIENCY   SOLUTION

Body Position

STROKE DEFICIENCY	SOLUTION
Top shoulder rolled forward or backward.	Roll shoulder backward or forward until body is perpendicular to water.
Body not sreamlined, bent at waist or hips.	Stretch the body from the top of the head to the toes during the glide.
Legs dropped too deep.	Lower head into water, or stop glide sooner and begin stroke.
Mouth under water.	Point top of head in direction of movement, lay head on lower shoulder.
Bottom arm too deep.	Stretch the bottom arm forward and keep it near the surface.

Bottom Arm Action

Bobbing motion of head and shoulders.

Bend elbow sooner during the force phase, keep side of head cushioned in the water.

Pulling, pushing motion for force and recovery phases.

Streamline during recovery by tucking elbow into the side and sliding the palm of the hand under the ear.

Top Arm Action

Arm too far from body on force and recovery.

Keep hand in contact with body during both phases.

Arm drifts past thigh at the end of the force phase.

Stop top arm at top of thigh as force phase is completed

Leg Action

Inverted scissors kick used.

Move top leg forward in the scissors kick.

Toes are pointed during entire kick resulting in lack of power.

Maintain a hooked (dorsal flexed) position until near the end of the force phase.

Legs move in an up and down plane (whip kick).

Move legs in a forward and backward direction parallel to water surface.

Legs cross each other at end of stroke.

Keep feet from drifting past each other, hold ankles together.

Coordination

Top arm recovers before the bottom arm can begin the force phase.

Get body in proper body position for start of stroke with top arm down on the thigh. Move both arms at the same time.

Glide too short or too long.

Start new stroke when the body momentum starts decreasing. New stroke starts before momentum stops.

FRONT CRAWL

This stroke is frequently referred to as the *"freestyle"*. It is performed in the prone position with the face in the water. This necessitates a need for developing a rhythmic breathing pattern. This stroke uses an over water recovery of the arms along with an up and down action of the legs. The arms work alternately so that one arm is always exerting force against the water. Since there is no glide, this is the fastest and most efficient stroke known to man.

Starting Body Position

The body is in a face down or prone position, almost parallel to the surface of the water. The body is straight, with the hips and legs slightly lower in the water than the head. The hairline marks the water level for the head.

Flutter Kick (Prone)

The leg action used in this stroke is called the flutter kick. It is characterized by an alternating, continuous undulating action of the legs. The object of the kick is to push the water backward with each leg swing. The action of the leg kick originates from the hip joint. A summation of forces of the joint action at the knee and ankle produces the power. This results in a whipping action of the feet.

Most of the power is generated on the upbeat or force phase of each leg stroke. The swimmer should avoid an attempt to exert a great deal of force on the downbeat of the kick, since this is the recovery phase of the kick. Excessive pressure against the water during the downbeat may retard forward motion.

During the force phase, the leg swings upward with the back (posterior) surface of the leg and sole of the foot on an angle effective enough to direct the force in a backward direction. The knee is flexed slightly at the beginning of the stroke. The ankle also flexes as it reacts to the weight of the water against it. Relaxing the foot will produce a natural toe-in effect, which is desirable. As the leg continues its upward swing, it gains momentum from the quick extension of the ankle and knee. The heel breaks the surface slightly and a bubbling action is created on the surface.

On the downbeat of the leg or recovery phase there is a less favorable angle for applying force. The front (anterior) surface of the leg produces force in a forward and downward direction which negates an effective backward force against the water. The knee is passively flexed and the ankle is passively extended during this phase. This is a good time for the legs to relax and prepare for the thrust upward or force phase.

The effectiveness of the kick depends on the length of a person's legs as well as the speed and depth of the kick. A shallow kick is best for the speed swimmer and one with short legs. For one with long legs or for a moderately paced stroke, let the foot drop 15 to 20 inches below the surface during the downbeat.

Arm Motion

The arms move in opposition through a force and recovery phase similar to the action of a windmill. By using a constant alternating action, the arms execute a constant force to pull the body forward by pushing water back toward the feet.

During the force phase the hand describes an "S" shaped path as it moves through the water. The force phase begins with one arm entering the water in line with the shoulder. The arm is rotated slightly inward (medially) at the shoulder joint and the elbow is bent and elevated above the wrist. This allows the fingers and hand to slide into the water first. The arm muscles contract as the palm enters the water.

As the arm begins its pull, it is important to keep the elbow up. Dropping the elbow will result in an inefficient stroke and a drastic reduction in the amount of force produced. Force is directed down and back as elbow flexion increases gradually. During this phase, the hand moves under the body and toward the midline. When the elbow reaches a point under the shoulder, the palm and forearm continue the pushing action as the elbow extends. The path of the thrust is back toward the outer border of the hip. As the hand approaches the hip it provides a final thrust back to release the water it was moving.

The final push of the hand in the force phase initiates the recovery phase. The elbow will break through the surface first, moving forward while the hand is completing the upsweep. In a slightly flexed position, the elbow travels upward and forward with the hand following. The palm is rotated inward as it leaves the water. As the hand passes the shoulder, the elbow begins to extend. The elbow continues to extend until the hand enters the water in front of the shoulder. The palm rotates outward as the hand enters the water with the fingers slightly spread.

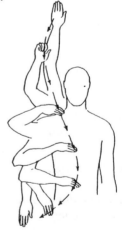

Front crawl underwater stroke pattern

Body roll is necessary for efficient stroke performance. The roll should be approximately 40 degrees on the breathing side and 25 degrees on the non-breathing side.

Breathing Cycle

Breathing should always occur on the same side, each swimmer decides which side to breathe on based on comfort. The head rests with the hairline at water level. This position is maintained throughout the rotation of the head. An air pocket is created at surface level on both sides of the head. This is caused by the swimmer's head cutting through the water like the bow of a ship. This bow wave or water depression allows the swimmer to breathe with minimal head rotation. As the head rotates into the air pocket formed by the bow wave, the swimmer takes a quick bite of air. Upon rotating the head back into the water, the exhalation phase begins. This phase continues until the head turns back into the air pocket.

Exhalation is accomplished by breathing out through the mouth and nose while the face is in the water. Holding the breath during the exhalation phase of the stroke will prevent the swimmer from taking in sufficient air during inhalation.

The breathing cycle for the crawl consists of a pattern of inhalation and exhalation completed during one stroke cycle. Inhalation occurs as the head rotates to one side. Exhalation occurs as the head rotates back down into the water.

Coordination of Stroke

Using a six beat crawl kick and a continuous arm action, the stroke coordination can be described in a six count rhythmic cycle. Individual body structures, the speed of the stroke and the level of competition may cause the number of beats of the kick to vary considerably. The six count cycle would be as follows:

Count 1 — Begin the force phase of arm one and the recovery of arm two while taking a bite of air. Execute one flutter kick.

Counts — Finish the force phase of arm one and the recovery phase of 2 & 3   arm two while exhaling in the water. Execute two flutter kicks.

Count 4 — Arm two begins the force phase of the stroke while arm one begins its recovery. Take a bite of air. Execute one flutter kick.

Counts — Finish the force phase of arm two and the recovery of arm 5 & 6   one while exhaling in the water. Execute two flutter kicks.

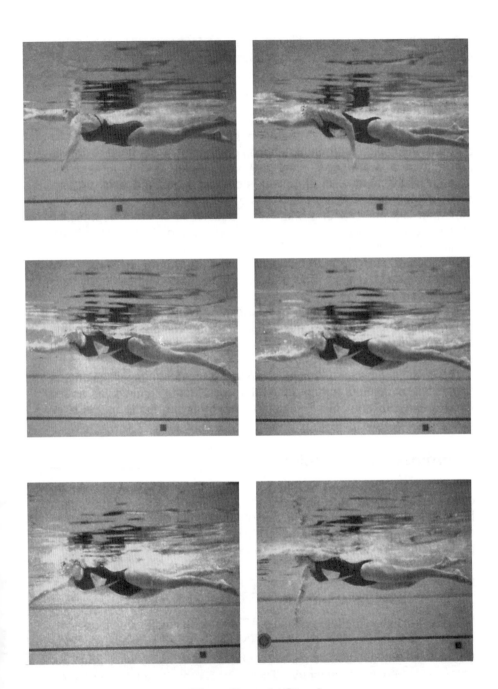

The Crawl Stroke

TROUBLESHOOTING THE CRAWL

STROKE DEFICIENCY   SOLUTION

Body Position

STROKE DEFICIENCY	SOLUTION
Chin tucks dropping head down, arm recovery and breathing are difficult.	Adjust head position so that the hairline is at water level.
Neck extends raising head too high, legs and hips drop too low.	Drop head to hairline level level in the water.

Leg Action

STROKE DEFICIENCY	SOLUTION
Excessive bending of the kicking power and fatigue.	Straighten legs slightly loss of and think of kicking a ball up to the surface with the sole of the foot.
Thighs never passing producing a very shallow kick with no pushing force.	Kick at least 10" deep.
Deep ineffective kick which causes fatigue.	Kick the depth of a walking stride, not a giant step.
Uneven kicking rhythm.	Practice on kickboards until it becomes effective and automatic.
Breaking the surface with the feet.	Check for low head, lift head slightly to drop legs.

Arm Action

STROKE DEFICIENCY	SOLUTION
Forearm hits water on entry before hand causing body to lift out of water.	Raising elbow and wrist above hand will decrease forearm resistance.
Ending force phase abruptly under the shoulder line making a short, choppy, stroke.	Keep eyes open to make sure force phase continues down the body to hip line or tiring starting point.

A stiff arm on recovery eliminates needed rest of the arm and hand muscle before the force phase.

Concentrate on keeping the arm and hand muscles relaxed as elbow lifts and in recovery.

Hands enter water too close to the head causing short, choppy strokes.

Open eyes underwater to see where hands enter.

Fingers cupped, wrist stiff.

Relax hands and wrist.

Pulling with straight arm resulting in inefficient force phase.

Use the "S" pattern with a high elbow as the arm pulls through.

Hand enters the water in front of the opposite shoulder causing the body to move diagonally through the water.

Hand should enter the water in line with the shoulder on the same side of the body.

Breathing

Holding breath creates tension and hyperventilation and no rhythmic breathing.

Begin to exhale as soon as the face enters the water after inhalation.

Lifting the head for breath causes a lowering of legs and difficult arm recovery.

Keep check on non-breathing side in the water during inhalation phase.

Rotating shoulders too much causes excessive rolling and impedes progress.

Rotate shoulders no more than 45 degrees on breathing side and 25 degrees on other side.

Water enters nose.

Exhale through mouth and nose with face in water.

Coordination

Breathing too soon or too late causes tension and excessive trunk action.

Inhalation begins at moment recovery of arm on breathing side starts.

Resting on the arm as it enters the water delays start of the force phase.

Develop a rhythm for the stroke with no pause or glide. It may be fast or slow, like the beat of a drum.

Breathing too late, resulting in insufficient air intake.

Inhalation must be complete by the time the elbow of the recovery arm passes the shoulder.

Excessive body roll toward breathing side causes uneven stroke.

Breathe later and cut down on the amount of shoulder roll.

BREASTSTROKE

The breaststroke, the elementary backstroke and the side stroke are the three resting strokes. They are referred to as resting strokes because each has a glide phase in which no propulsion occurs. These strokes are slower than the crawl stroke which has continuous arm and leg movements.

Starting Body Position

A prone or face down position, almost horizontal to the surface of the water is used for this stroke. The legs are together with the toes pointed. The face is in the water to hairline level. The arms are extended at surface level in front of the head with the hands close together.

Arm Motion

The arm motion for the breaststroke consists of an outsweep, catch, downsweep, insweep, and a recovery. In the outsweep, the palms of the hands turn outward and the outstretched arms sweep directly outward slightly beyond shoulder width.

The catch is made by flexing the wrists so that the palms face downward. The direction of the hands changes from outward to downward.

The downsweep begins with the elbows flexing, while staying high in the water near the surface. The hands pull forcefully out and down into the water back toward the feet.

During the insweep the hands continue to circle downward and inward and upward until just prior to the recovery phase. As the hands pass under the elbows, they change their pitch from an outward to an inward position. The upward motion of the hands lowers the hips, and the knees are then able to initiate leg recovery. This completes the force phase of the breaststroke.

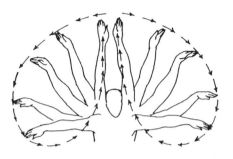 

Breaststroke underwater stroke pattern

The recovery phase of the arms is composed of a hand-elbow-hand movement. To begin, the hands come together. The elbows collapse into the body or move downward and inward. Finally, the hands meet under the chin and the palms turn down and forward as the elbows extend.

Whip Kick (Prone)

The whip kick used in the breaststroke provides a large portion of the propulsion for the stroke. Unlike the up and down motions of the flutter kick used in the crawl and back crawl, this kick makes a movement out to the side, around, and down. This kick is also used in the elementary back stroke. Competitive swimmers may choose to combine a dolphin type kick with it for greater propulsion.

The wedge kick or frog kick is similar to the whip kick with the exception that the knees are outside of the feet instead of inside when the force phase begins. This kick is no longer preferred by the American Red Cross for teaching beginning and intermediate swimmers. However, it is still used for teaching older adults who have lost knee flexibility due to arthritis or knee surgery.

The legs are together, knees straight and toes pointed when the recovery phase of the kick begins. As the knees flex and drop and the heels move toward the buttocks, the thighs remain together. When the knees are at the lowest point, the feet turn outward and the knees part slightly. With the bottom of the feet facing backward, the legs are poised for the force phase or whipping action of the kick.

The force phase of the kick is initiated as the legs begin a whip like action in a backward direction. Forcing the water backwards gives the body forward impetus. The inside of the legs and bottom of the feet serve as agents of force to execute the whip. The kick ends with both legs straight and together with toes pointed.

Coordination of Stroke and Breathing Cycle

The inhalation phase begins just as the extended arms part and travel in the outsweep phase of the force of the arms. The head which has been submerged to hairline level lifts until the nose clears the water. As air is inhaled the arms continue in the force phase. The legs begin to recover. When the elbows collapse to the sides of the body and the hands come together, the head submerges to prepare for the thrust of the legs created by the whip kick.

With the head lowered only to hairline level, the arms extend to a fully outstretched position with the fingers pointed. Exhalation begins at the beginning of the force phase of the leg stroke and the recovery phase of the arm stroke. It continues through the glide portion of the stroke. It is important for the swimmer to blow air out the entire time in order to be ready for a breath when the force phase of the arm begins the downsweep.

For stroke coordination, several cue words can be used.

PULL — (arms pull), inhale

AND BREATHE — (arms recover to sides) legs recover

KICK — (arms extend forward), legs kick, exhale

GLIDE — (body is in streamlined straight position with legs and arms together) exhale.

The main words to learn are *Pull and Breathe, Kick, Glide.* It is desirable to practice the arm action and kick action first before coordinating breathing with the stroke.

The Breaststroke

TROUBLESHOOTING THE BREASTSTROKE

STROKE DEFICIENCY   SOLUTION

Body Position

Arching the back causes the trunk to sink and lower back strain.

Re-align body into near horizontal position, stretch during glide.

Turning body to side creates scissors kick.

Keep body prone and the hips flat near the surface.

Dropping the head too low or holding it too high contributes to poor arm action and inaccurate leg position in water.

Coordinate breathing with arm cycle, keep head at hairline during long exhalation period.

Arm Action

Arms pull all the way to the thigh because of weak kick, throws timing off and makes arm recovery difficult.

Shorten pull, end arm downsweep when hands are just below the shoulders. Lift head sooner to inhale.

Leading with palms or back of the hands in recovery.

A fingertip lead decreases drag.

Dropping the elbows too soon in the force phase of the stroke.

Keep elbows high until the hands come in line with them at the end of the downsweep.

Leg Action

Pulling the knees too far under the body in recovery pushes the hips out of the water.

Be sure the heels stay near the surface as the knees bend.

Heels move outside of the knees causing a frog kick.

Keep knees in line with the hips and keep the heels wider than the knees.

Pointing toes early in the force phase weakens kick.

Keep feet flexed and push with the soles of the feet.

Knees too close together during force phase decreases power.

Knees should be about 10"-12" or shoulder width apart at beginning of force phase.

Fast recovery inhibits forward movement.

Recover legs slowly to decrease resistance.

Dipping one shoulder or hip may cause a scissor like kick.

Keep the body almost flat and parallel to the surface of the water, recover legs symmetrically.

Coordination and Breathing

Pulling arms and legs at the same time produces a total loss of coordination.

Use cue words for coordination: PULL, KICK, AND, GLIDE.

With no glide, coordination is off within two or three strokes.

Glide for two to three seconds at the end of the stroke.

Lifting the head too high out of the water to inhale produces a bobbing effect thus an inefficient stroke.

A good arm pull lifts the head out of the water sufficiently to obtain a bite of air, lower head only to hairline level.

Holding the breath for several strokes produces fatigue.

Breathe every stroke for ease and comfort, unless in training for competition.

Breathing too early or too late produces ineffective coordination.

Lift the head to breathe as the hands start to separate at the beginning of the force phase.

BACK CRAWL

The back crawl is also called the backstroke, a term most used for competitive purposes. Both the front and back crawl use a continuous, alternating over the water arm recovery and a flutter kick. These strokes are very similar; however, the front crawl is performed in a prone position and the back crawl in a supine or back position. Since the body is in a different position, many of the techniques differ in their execution. The crawl strokes are faster and more strenuous than the three resting strokes.

Starting Body Position

The body is extended in a back glide position. The back of the head is submerged to about ear level. The hips and legs are slightly lower than the trunk to permit an effective kick. The shoulders are at water level. Eyes should be focused toward the toes or beyond for assistance in keeping the body swimming in a straight line.

Flutter Kick (Supine)

The flutter kick in the back crawl is similar to the kick that was used in the front crawl. It is a continuous, alternating undulating action of the legs in the water with a force and recovery phase.

The novice swimmer may think of the kicking action as punting a football with the top of the foot meeting the ball just out of the water. Leg action originates at the hip joint. This is followed by sequential joint action of the knees and ankles. The recovery phase is started when the knees bend and the feet drop down in the water. The action must be strong enough to overcome water resistance, but not strong enough to create a negative force which would pull the body backward toward the feet. The knee and ankle remain passive and slightly flexed until near the end of the downswing. At the end of the downswing, the foot may be from 15 to 20 inches below the surface of the water.

The force of the flutter kick in the back crawl is gained on the upswing of each leg. As the leg begins the force phase, it exposes the front (anterior) surface of the lower leg and the top of the foot to direct the force in a backward direction. The knees are flexed prior to the lift and the toes turn toward the midline of the body. The leg continues to thrust upward and gains momentum until fully extended. This action carries the foot upward for the final whip like action as the toes break the surface of the water. The transition to the recovery phase occurs as the leg muscles momentarily relax before starting the downswing.

Arm Motion

The alternating force and recovery action of the arm stroke is similar to that of the crawl. The recovery action lifts the arm from the water and carries it to the point of entry for the force phase. The recovery phase commences with the arm extended against the side of the body below the surface. The arm lifts from the water with the wrist and elbow fairly straight. The thumb leads and the palm faces inward as the arm lifts straight up and over the shoulder. As the arm passes the shoulder line, the hand turns to a little finger leading, palm outward position while reaching backward for the water. The hand enters the water just outside the shoulder line or at a one or eleven o'clock position (depending upon the arm used).

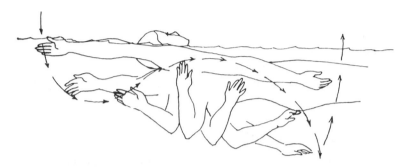

Backcrawl underwater stroke pattern

The force phase begins as the hand enters the water with the little finger leading and the palm facing outward. The arm slices to a depth of 10 to 12 inches with the shoulder rotating down into the water. The head is held straight.

The first part of the force phase is called the *catch*. Following the catch, the pull begins. The entire pull has been described as a question mark (?) pattern. Shortly after the pull begins, the elbow starts to bend as the arm and hand sink deeper in the water due to the shoulder roll. As the elbow bends, the upper arm rotates to prevent the elbow from dropping. With the hand directly opposite the shoulder, the elbow bend will be approximately 90 degrees. The hand comes within a few inches of the top of the water. After maximum elbow bend, the hand pushes downward in a quarter circle motion. The elbow extends as the palm pushes over and toward the bottom of the pool. This final thrust causes the body to roll on its longitudinal axis in preparation for the recovery phase.

Coordination of Stroke and Breathing Cycle

Nearly all back crawl swimmers use a six beat kick. There should be three beats per armstroke or six beats per arm cycle. Breathing naturally and rhythmically is suggested for the back crawl since the face is out of the water the entire time.

The timing of the arms is the main concern in coordination. The important principle to remember is that the arms do not rest, but move in a continuous cycle. As one arm is recovering, the other is pulling. A helpful suggestion may be to vocalize the rhythm of the stroke by saying "LIFT, TWO, THREE". The word "lift" is better than "pull" since the common error is the delay of recovery in the arm stroke.

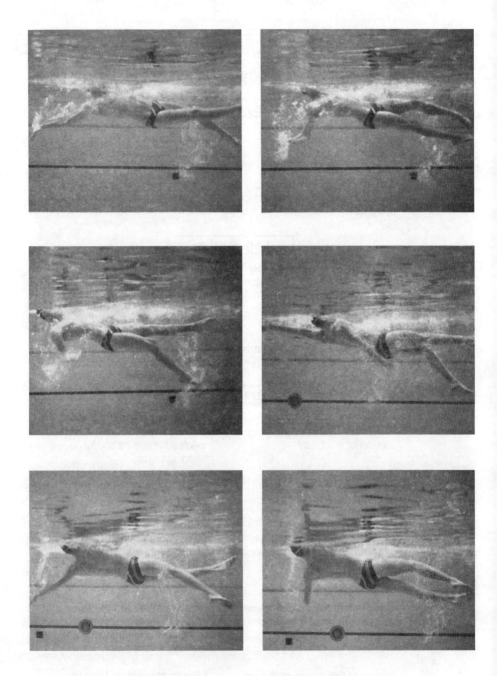

The Back Crawl Stroke

TROUBLESHOOTING THE BACK CRAWL

STROKE DEFICIENCY   SOLUTION

Body Position

If head is low or high in the water, the kick will be ineffective.

Tuck chin slightly and look toward the feet, keep back of head in the water.

Sitting in the water will drop the hips and create resistance progress.

Stretch body longitudinally to a straight back glide position.

Leg Action

Knees bend excessively on upbeat, too much out of water action, loss of power.

Straighten knees as leg and foot force water toward the surface, spray should be no more than 6".

Bending knees forcefully on downbeat causes negative thrust of body.

Initiate leg action from hips.

Arm Action

Hand enters water inside shoulder line causing zigzag motion of the body.

Hands enter water just outside shoulder line. Shoulder follows for the catch, keep head straight.

Pausing as the hand enters the water causes loss of momentum.

Use momentum of recovery phase to catch and pull during force phase.

Using straight arm for underwater stroke causes the upper body to rise in the water.

By the time the hand pulls to shoulder level, the elbow should be at a 90 degree angle for the push.

Failing to turn the palm downward at the end of the force phase prevents shoulder elevation for recovery phase.

Turn the palm down at the end of the force phase as the arm is extended along the side of the body.

Swinging the arm over the top of the body causes water to be sprayed in the face.

Lift arm straight up from the side of the body to enter the water slightly outside of the shoulder.

A stiff arm recovery does not let the muscles rest and the force phase becomes weak.	Slight elbow and wrist flexion at the beginning of recovery relieves tension in the arms.

Coordination

When one arm moves and the other is stationary, the body zigzags and the force of the stroke is diminished.	Move both arms in a continuous motion but in opposition. One lifts from the water as the other enters. Say "Lift, 2, 3" to help keep the rhythm.
Moving the recovery arm faster than the pulling arm destroys the rhythm of the stroke.	Coordination requires that the speed of the recovery arm be the same as that of the pulling arm. Use cue words or count.

ADAPTATIONS FOR THE DISABLED

Swimming is for everyone, including those who are unable to perform all the techniques as they have been described due to body differences. The college student who takes swimming and has a disability should discuss the ramifications of his limitations with the instructor.

The following are some suggestions for adaptations of the five basic strokes for different disability groups. There is no attempt to relate the etiology, symptoms, and characteristics of each. The American Red Cross has published *Adapted Aquatics* which may be of assistance to both the student and the instructor in this regard.

The orthopedically impaired student may have one to four limbs affected. Those with only one limb affected (monoplegic) will not have too much difficulty in swimming any of the strokes. The kick will need to be changed to a strong, slow flutter or to the positive action of the scissors kick by first reaching forward and then reaching backward with one good leg. Paraplegics (two limbs affected, usually the legs) can swim the back strokes because they usually have no trouble floating on their backs. For a prone stroke, the breaststroke may be best. For the breaststroke, use a short continuous pull without a glide. The crawl and side strokes may be difficult without a good kick. If arm strength is good, a back butterfly is possible.

A hemiplegic (paralyzed on one side of the body) should breathe over the weak shoulder in the crawl. The side stroke can be accomplished with the good or heavy side down, if a good scissors kick can be adapted. A flotation device should be used only if the student cannot use his own buoyancy to maintain proper body position.

Students with muscular dystrophy will usually learn to float. The elementary back stroke will be easiest, although it may have to be modified. A finning action of the hands and kicking up with the feet may drain all the strength available. If the individual is strong enough, a breaststroke using only the arms may be attempted.

A neuromuscular impaired person may have cerebral palsy. Ataxic and athetoid cerebral palsied students can usually learn the elementary back stroke. This is because the arm and leg action can be performed simultaneously. First, learn the arm action, then the leg action before coordinating it into a complete stroke.

Visually impaired students have been known to be very competitive on swimming teams. A beginning student, however, will need tactile guidance on land, and in the water. The use of good verbal cues along with the manual movement of the body parts in the water helps the student learn the strokes. A book entitled *Aquatic Recreation for the Blind* by Harry C. Cordellos is a helpful reference for those dealing with the blind student in an aquatic activity.

Hearing impaired students can learn to swim well, if instructions are given clearly enough for lip reading or if the instructor can communicate in sign language. Ear molds can be worn for protection of the ears while in the water. Films showing above water and underwater views of strokes and parts of strokes are excellent visual aids. Some colleges have underwater windows where the hearing impaired person can see the action.

Learning disabled students can learn all the strokes in their entirety. Their need is to hear and understand the instructions clearly before attempting the arm and leg actions. The instructor needs to be patient because their attention span is short and explanations may have to be given several times.

Heart patients, epileptics, and asthmatics can learn the elementary backstroke without fear of mild or severe attacks due to the face-up position and relaxed nature of the stroke. The other four major strokes can be learned as well, if the students have managed to control their disabilities with medicine or in other ways.

As a general rule, the elementary backstroke is the best stroke to begin teaching the disabled student. If the student can float on the back, adapting the stroke to make it efficient should not be difficult. In most cases, the breaststroke is the best stroke to teach in a prone position. A good arm press and the ability to hyperextend the neck for a breath of air is all that is needed.

SUMMARY

A swimmer must be aware of the effects of water resistance when attempting to develop an efficient stroke. By understanding resistance, he should be able to reduce its negative effects. A swimmer should also have some knowledge of Newton's Laws as they apply to swimming.

The five basic strokes are the elementary backstroke, sidestroke, breaststroke, front crawl and back crawl. The first three strokes listed above are frequently referred to as resting strokes due to the pause or glide that is part of each stroke. The last two strokes are continuous strokes which allow for faster swimming, but tire the swimmer more quickly.

Most strokes can be adapted for individuals who have a variety of handicapping conditions. Since there are so many causes and differences in the severity of disabilities, the teacher and student must work together in order to develop the best possible stroke in a given situation. Some suggestions for possible adaptations have been given in this chapter.

REVIEW QUESTIONS

1. If a swimmer's legs drop too low in the water, which type of resistance would be experienced as a result?

2. Discuss Newton's Third Law in the following situation.

   A swimmer using the elementary backstroke has difficulty swimming in a straight line. The swimmer's body keeps turning to the left.

3. What would probably cause an individual who is practicing the flutter kick in a prone position to remain stationary in the water or possibly move backwards? How can this be corrected?

4. Explain the timing for the breaststroke.

5. What must be done to streamline the body when swimming the sidestroke? Why is this necessary?

SELECTED REFERENCES

1. American National Red Cross. (1977). *Adapted Aquatics*. Washington, DC: American National Red Cross.

2. American National Red Cross. (1974). *Manual for the Basic Swimming Instructor*. Washington, DC: American National Red Cross.

3. American National Red Cross. (1981). *Swimming and Aquatic Safety.* Washington, DC: American National Red Cross.

4. Bland, H., (1979). *Competitive Swimming.* England: E. P. Publishing, Ltd.

5. Collis, M. & Kirchoff, B., (1974). *Swimming.* Boston: Allyn and Bacon.

6. Jones, J. A., (1988). *Teaching Guide to Cerebral Palsy Sports.* (3rd ed.) Champaign, IL: Human Kinetics.

7. Maglischo, E. W., (1982). *Swimming Faster.* Palo Alto, CA: Mayfield.

8. Maglischo, E. W. & Brennan, C. F., (1985). *Swim for the Health of It.* Palo Alto, CA: Mayfield.

9. Midtlyng, J., (1982). *Swimming.* (2nd ed.) Philadelphia, PA: Saunders.

10. Prins, J., (1982). *The Illustrated Swimmer.* Honolulu, HI: Honolulu He'e Vickers.

11. B. J. & Vincent, W. J., (1984). *Swimming.* (4th ed.) Dubuque, IA: Wm. C. Brown.

12. Young Men's Christian Assn., (1986). *YMCA Progressive Swimming "Splash".* Champaign, IL: Human Kinetics.

13. Young Men's Christian Assn., (1986). *YMCA Progressive Swimming Instructor's Guide.* Champaign, IL: Human Kinetics.

CHAPTER 8

Mobility Skills For The Novice Swimmer

An individual is ready to learn a series of techniques for improving mobility in the water after becoming comfortable in the water and learning one or more basic swimming strokes. The skills discussed in this chapter will help the student to maneuver above and below the surface of the water.

Although some of the skills in this chapter such as turning over, changing directions, sculling and treading water are sometimes taught earlier, a decision was made to place them later in this text. This was done in an effort to assemble skills together in a logical grouping. There was no intention to teach every student five strokes prior to teaching any of these skills. An individual instructor may introduce these skills in a different order.

Skills discussed in this chapter will help to develop the student's confidence in learning to be more at home in the water. Other skills include: underwater swimming, three types of surface dives and open turns.

TURNING OVER

A swimmer who gets tired while swimming in the prone position may want to roll over into a supine position to continue swimming. Turning from a face down to a face up position is a very important skill that can be learned once the prone and back kick glides have been mastered.

A very simple technique can be used to turn the body 180 degrees on its longitudinal axis. Push off into a prone kick glide with the arms together overhead. Turn the head to the left, move the left shoulder backward along with the left hip. Once the turn is initiated, continue the momentum created by the head, shoulder and hip until the turn has been completed. Keep the body straight and the hips up and begin kicking. A roll to the right would be initiated by turning the head to the right.

Turning over from the back to the front, or supine to prone, can be more difficult. The chief problem that occurs with beginners is dropping the hips to facilitate the turn. This causes the swimmer to sink. The best way to rotate the body from a face-up to face-down position is to think of the body as a "hot dog" turning over on the grill to cook. With both arms overhead or with both arms at the side of the body, turn over as a single unit. Initiate this action with the head, followed by the shoulders, then the hips. Take a deep breath before going into the face-down position. Once the turn has been completed, move the body forward with the legs as in the prone kick glide, or with both arms and legs as in the beginning stroke or crawl stroke.

CHANGING DIRECTIONS

The ability to change directions is an important skill for any swimmer. This skill is essential to those who swim in open bodies of water as well as those who swim in pools. Those who swim into deep water use this skill to easily return to the shore or the side of the pool.

Changing directions is like making a "U Turn". The swimmer begins by swimming the crawl or breaststroke out from the side of the pool. To go back, the swimmer moves his head in the direction of the turn. If the turn is to the right, shorten the stroke with the right arm and reach further to the right than normal with the left arm. After completing the turn, swim back to the starting point.

CHANGING POSITIONS

Another useful skill is changing positions in the water. This is the ability to move from a vertical to a horizontal position.

To change from a horizontal to a vertical position, the student should lift the head, draw the knees toward the chest and press down against the water with the arms. Once in the vertical position, the legs should be extended toward the bottom. If in deep water, tread water to remain afloat. (Treading water is described later in this chapter.)

To move from a vertical position into a horizontal prone position, the student should first drop the head forward, and draw the knees to the chest. The arms are swept in a forward, upward direction from a position along side of the body. When the body has rotated to a face down position, the legs are extended backward at the surface of the water. From this prone position the student is ready to begin swimming or to roll over on the back.

SCULLING

Sculling is a skill which involves the use of the hands and forearms to propel the body through the water. It is also used in treading water and in performing various figures in synchronized swimming. To learn the sculling action, start by standing in waist deep water. Keeping the elbows close to the sides, rest the palms and forearms on the surface of the water, about twelve inches apart. Rotate the palms inward (supinate) so that the thumbs are lifted slightly out of the water. Draw the palms toward each other. Rotate the palms in the opposite direction (pronate) so that the thumbs are in the water and the little fingers are out of the water. Push the hands in an outward direction until they are about twelve inches apart. Repeat this figure-8 pattern, moving the arms and hands more quickly. As skill is increased, the amount of rotation can be decreased.

Once the sculling action has been learned, it can be performed while in the prone float or back float position. Float in a supine (back) position with the hands close to the hips. Using the sculling action described above (a flat scull) the body should remain stationary in the water. To cause the body to move through the water in the direction of the head, continue the sculling action; but change the angle of the wrist so that it is hyperextended. To move toward the feet, scull with the wrists flexed.

One method of sculling while in the prone float position is called a canoe scull. This is performed with the hands under the hips. The wrists are hyperextended as the sculling action is performed. This will cause the body to move in a forward direction.

TREADING WATER

Treading water is a personal safety skill. It is used to keep the face out of the water in order to facilitate breathing while the body is in a vertical position. Treading water is accomplished by using a sculling action with the hands along with a leg kick.

To practice, kneel in waist deep water. Start with the elbows close to the sides, fingers pointing forward, palms down. The hands should be approximately twelve inches apart and deep in the water (about waist level). Begin a strong, quick sculling action. If the sculling action is sufficient, the body should rise from the bottom. Continue to hold the body up by sculling.

Either a scissors kick or a whip kick can be used in treading water. The student should choose the kick which he feels is the most powerful. Hold on to the side of the pool to practice the kick in deep water while in a vertical position. Keep the legs moving continuously. Once the student has tried both kicks and determined which is the most effective, he can practice using the sculling action of the arms with the selected kick.

UNDERWATER SWIMMING

The ability to swim underwater may come in handy when trying to retrieve an item that has been dropped into the water. It is an important lifesaving and rescue technique and is necessary for those interested in snorkeling and scuba diving.

Although no specific form has been defined for underwater swimming, a modified version of the breaststroke pull is most frequently used. One of several kicks can be used. The swimmer may elect to use the whip kick, the scissors kick or the flutter kick. The choice of a specific kick is based on the amount of power the swimmer gets from each of the kicks or on the purpose for swimming underwater (i.e., scuba diving with fins requires a modified flutter kick).

Take a deep breath and submerge below the surface of the water near the end of the pool. Use the feet to push off the end wall with the arms extended as in the glide position in the breaststroke. Drop the head in order to help keep the body below the surface of the water.

Once under the water, pull the arms back as in the breaststroke. Modify the pull by pressing the hands and forearms all the way back to the hips. In this position, allow the body to glide for a short distance.

The arms are recovered by drawing them up along the body. The hands meet at about chin level. Then the arms are extended out in front of the head ready to begin another pull without pausing.

If the whip kick or scissors kick is used, kick as the arms recover. If the flutter kick is used, kick continuously throughout the stroke.

The swimmer should exhale small amounts of air periodically through the mouth and nose while under water. If there is a problem staying under the water, try dropping the head, flexing the hips or pushing water upward during the pull. The swimmer should keep the eyes open underwater so that straight forward progress can be made and underwater objects can be avoided.

HYPERVENTILATION

Hyperventilation is a dangerous practice which is used by some swimmers to increase the time they are able to remain beneath the surface of the water. Some swimmers attempt to increase the ability to hold their breath by taking a number of deep breaths. In so doing, large amounts of carbon dioxide are exhaled. This reduces the amount of carbon dioxide in the blood. Because of the reduced amount of carbon dioxide, the individual is able to swim a greater distance before the carbon dioxide level is increased sufficiently to provide a strong breathing stimulus.

The problem lies in the fact that the swimmer may lose consciousness (black out) before the carbon dioxide level is sufficient enough to create a strong urge to breathe. Drowning may occur unless the individual is quickly pulled from the water.

In a recent case, after most everyone had left, a lifeguard hyperventilated in attempting to see how many lengths of the pool he could swim underwater. He passed out and was lying on the bottom when two young girls happened to see him. They jumped in, brought him up, and one performed rescue breathing while the other went for help. He lived. However, had no one seen him, he would have drowned as a result of hyperventilation.

SURFACE DIVES

The surface dive is a technique which is used to go from the surface of the water to a point beneath the surface. It can be either a headfirst or a feet-first technique. It is used for making rescues in lifesaving, retrieving a lost item, getting below the surface in scuba diving and as a figure in synchronized swimming. Surface dives may be performed in one of three different positions: feet-first, pike, or tuck.

Feet-first Surface Dive

The feet-first surface dive is used when the swimmer needs to submerge in dark, murky water of unknown depth or when bottom conditions are not known. The swimmer must rotate the body into a vertical position in the water in preparation for performing this technique.

Begin by moving the arms to a position straight out from the sides of the body and on the surface of the water. The palms of the hands should face downward. Firmly press the arms through the water and down to the sides. At the same time, kick the legs using either a scissors or a whip kick. This will raise the upper body out of the water. With the legs together, the body then will sink down under the water.

When the head has sunk below the surface, turn the palms outward (supinate), and use the arms to forcefully press upward against the water. Change the position of the body in order to swim in a forward direction after submerging to the desired depth. This can be done by dropping the head and pulling the knees to the chest. Roll forward, extend the legs behind the body and stretch the arms out in front of the body and begin swimming.

Pike Surface Dive

The pike surface dive is a head first dive from the surface of the water. It is used to get beneath the surface quickly to perform a rescue in deep water. It is the best head first surface dive to use when scuba diving or snorkeling.

It is easiest to begin the pike surface dive from a modified breaststroke. Lift the head to take a breath of air as the arms separate and begin pulling back toward the shoulders parallel to and just below the surface of the water. Continue moving the arms all the way back to the thighs.

Keeping the knees straight, drop the chin and flex the hips to move the upper body into a head down position, nearly perpendicular to the surface of the water. The hips are extended as the arms are pressed forward and downward toward the head with the elbows flexed and the palms down. This will facilitate the lifting of the legs by creating an equal and opposite reaction (arms moving down while the legs move up). The extension of the hips brings the legs to a vertical position well above the water, forcing the body straight down toward the bottom.

Once the swimmer reaches the desired depth, he should assume a horizontal position to swim in a forward direction. To prevent water from entering the nose on the descent, the swimmer should exhale continuously through the nostrils.

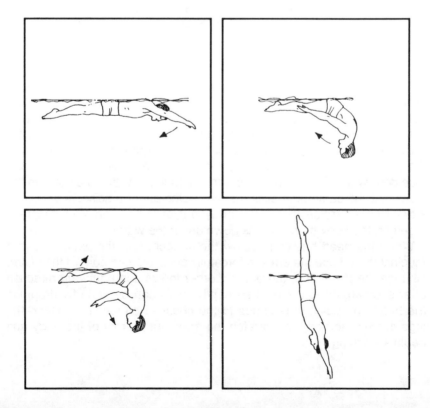

Tuck Surface Dive

The tuck surface dive is another variation of a head first surface dive. It differs from the pike surface dive in that the knees are bent or "tucked" during one phase of the technique. The tuck surface dive is frequently used by those who have difficulty lifting the legs off the surface of the water with the knees extended as in the pike surface dive. It is also a frequently used figure in synchronized swimming.

A modified breaststroke arm action is used to begin this technique. Lift the head to take a breath as the arms begin sweeping backward just below the surface of the water. Tuck the chin and draw the knees in close to the chest as the arms continue moving backward from the shoulders toward the thighs. This will cause the body to roll into a head down position with the feet and buttocks at the surface of the water.

Begin pressing the arms forward and downward toward the head with the elbows bent and the palms down. At the same time, quickly extend the legs straight upward out of the water. The weight of the extended legs will force the body down into the water. As in the pike surface dive, begin blowing air out during the descent and swim forward once the desired depth has been reached.

TURNS

Turns have been developed to give the swimmer an effective method of changing directions at the end of the pool. There are two types of turns which are used: open turns and closed turns. Open turns are used by the recreational swimmer while closed turns are used by the competitive swimmer. Open turns for the front crawl, sidestroke, breaststroke and back crawl will be described. Students interested in learning closed or flip turns should refer to a textbook on competitive swimming.

Front Crawl Turn

As the swimmer approaches the wall when swimming the front crawl, the lead arm touches the wall. The elbow of the lead arm bends as the momentum carries the body in closer to the wall. Then the swimmer lifts his head, tucks his legs and pulls them under his body. He turns away from the lead arm and places his feet on the wall one above the other 10-12 inches below the surface. The swimmer extends both arms out in front of his body and drops his head as the legs push off the wall in a side-lying, streamlined position. While exhailng through the nose the swimmer rolls to a face down position, gliding through the water. When the momentum from the push-off decreases, the kick begins. As the body reaches the surface, the arm stroke begins.

The Front Crawl Turn

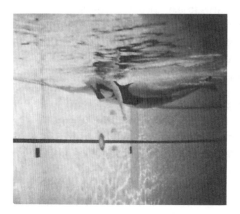

Sidestroke Turn

When the swimmer approaches the wall while swimming the sidestroke, the lead (bottom) arm touches first. The arm bends as the momentum from the last stroke carries the body closer to the wall. The legs are tucked and swung under the body and placed on the wall 12 to 15 inches below the surface. Leaning away from the wall, the swimmer drops the head into the water, and extends the arms to an overhead position while using the legs to push off the wall. After a brief glide, the top arm is pulled to the thigh, ready to begin the next stroke.

The above technique for the sidestroke turn is used when the swimmer swims to the wall on one side and wants to change sides for the next length of the pool. There is an alternate technique which will allow the swimmer to continue swimming on the same side. This technique is described below.

The swimmer approaches the wall and makes contact with the leading (bottom) arm. The elbow flexes as the body continues to move toward the wall. With the head lifted and knees drawn toward his chest, the swimmer turns toward the lead arm and places the other hand on the wall. The feet are placed on the wall 12 to 15 inches below the surface of the water. Both arms are extended overhead as the feet push off the wall with the body in a side gliding position. After a short glide, the top arm is pulled toward the thigh in preparation for beginning a stroke.

The Sidestroke Turn

Breaststroke Turn

In the breaststroke turn, the swimmer contacts the wall simultaneously with both hands. The elbows are bent and the knees are drawn up into a tuck position. The swimmer may turn either to the right or to the left. If the turn is to the right, the right arm drops away from the wall, the head drops toward the right shoulder and the feet are placed on the wall 10 to 12 inches below water level.

The left hand which is still touching the wall is thrown over the surface of the water to a point past the head. The swimmer rolls to a prone position with arms together overhead as the legs are used to push off the wall. He glides with arms and legs extended. The first arm pull after the glide will bring the swimmer to the surface.

The Breaststroke Turn

Back Crawl Turn

The backstroker contacts the wall with the leading arm which should be straight and in line with the shoulder. The leading arm bends as the knees are tucked. The swimmer pivots his body toward the leading arm and places the feet on the wall 12 to 15 inches below the surface. He brings both arms along side of the head with the elbows bent. As the arms are extended into a streamlined position, the swimmer pushes off underwater. The swimmer should glide for one to two seconds before beginning the kick.

The Back Crawl Turn

ADAPTATIONS FOR THE DISABLED

The hearing impaired student should not swim underwater unless ear protection is available. This is necessary to prevent the possibility of ear infections. Surface diving would also be contraindicated. Learning to do all other water adjustment skills is desirable.

The visually impaired student can learn all the skills contained in this chapter. The depth of the water for surface diving must be carefully monitored for fear of head injury. Verbal cues or manual instructor guidance through the water adjustment skills of turning over, changing directions and position, sculling, or treading water are all that are needed for success.

The orthopedically impaired student may have difficulty with treading water, if the lower limbs are involved. To tread effectively, a strong scull must be developed. A slight back-lying position will also help. The tuck or pike surface dive may be extremely difficult or even impossible, if the teacher expects the student to lift the legs off the surface of the water. The feet first surface dive may be easier and more appropriate.

A person with muscular dystrophy can do most of the water adjustment skills without extra help. A lack of upper body strength may prevent the accomplishment of surface diving. The sculling action of the arms should be strong for treading water.

The cerebral palsy student can learn to turn over by using the one good side or shoulder to assist in the maneuver. Underwater swimming can also be enjoyable once a means of propulsion with one or more limbs has been achieved. This would be a good experience to prepare for scuba diving activities.

All others with disabling conditions such as heart disease, epilepsy, and asthma should use the appropriate medicines to control the condition when in swimming classes. For the majority of disabled students, water adjustment skills could be accomplished with proper instruction and plenty of practice.

SUMMARY

The skills described in this chapter are essential for all swimmers. They are used in recreational swimming as well as in special activities such as scuba diving, synchronized swimming, snorkeling, lifesaving and rescue. Through the use of skills such as turning over, changing directions, treading water, sculling, underwater swimming, and others, the student will gain increased confidence as well as increased mobility in the water. It is desirable to be able to move in any direction: right, left, up or down. The beginner should also be able to change from a horizontal to a vertical position or from a prone to a supine position and vice versa. Learning these maneuvering skills in the water is necessary before mastering the basic strokes or attempting the advanced ones.

REVIEW QUESTIONS

1. Explain the statement, "The body follows the head", in relation to the following skills: turning over, changing directions, and the breaststroke turn.

2. How is it possible to change the direction in which the body moves while sculling?

3. Why is the feet-first surface dive started with a strong kick and a forceful downward pull of the arms?

4. How does the tuck surface dive differ from the pike surface dive?

5. Discuss the dangers of hyperventilation.

SELECTED REFERENCES

1. American National Red Cross. (1977). *Adapted Aquatics.* Washington, DC: American National Red Cross.

2. American National Red Cross. (1974). *Manual for the Basic Swimming Instructor.* Washington, DC: American National Red Cross.

3. American National Red Cross. (1981). *Swimming and Aquatic Safety.* Washington, DC: American National Red Cross.

4. Maglischo, E. W. & Brennan, C. F., (1985). *Swim for the Health of It.* Palo Alto, CA: Mayfield.

5. Whiting, H. T. A., (1970). *Teaching the Persistent Non-Swimmer.* London: G. Bell and Sons.

CHAPTER 9
Advanced Swimming Strokes

The strokes discussed in this chapter are not advanced strokes because of a difficulty rating, but because they are generally contained in advanced swimming courses. For instance, the overarm sidestroke which is discussed first is a very easy stroke to master once the basic sidestroke is learned. The only difference is that the top arm recovers out of the water instead of under the water. A novice swimmer could learn this stroke with little difficulty.

The term "advanced" is commonly used because the strokes are built upon the basic strokes. The overarm sidestroke and the inverted breaststroke require only minor changes in the basic strokes. The trudgen was the forerunner of the modern crawl. The butterfly was first introduced as a form of the breaststroke in which the breaststroke kick was used with the butterfly arm pull. In 1952, the International Federation of Amateur Swimmers was instrumental in making the breaststroke and butterfly two separate strokes.

The swimming strokes in this chapter are presented in a format similar to that used to describe the basic strokes in Chapter Seven. They are discussed in order of difficulty from the overarm sidestroke to the butterfly.

THE OVERARM SIDESTROKE

This stroke is similar to the basic sidestroke. Three limbs (the bottom arm and both legs) function in exactly the same way as in the regular sidestroke. The only difference is that the top arm makes an over water recovery similar to that of the crawl.

The beauty of this stroke is seen in synchronized swimming or water ballet routines. In the early days of competitive swimming, the overarm sidestroke was listed as an event. Now, it's just a lot of fun to swim!

Starting Body Position

Start in a side-lying position in the water. Extend the bottom arm straight up from the shoulder. The back of the head rests on that shoulder with the face tilted so that the mouth is out of the water for breathing purposes. The top arm is extended straight down the body from the shoulder with the hand resting on top of the thigh. The legs are together and fully extended with the toes pointed.

Bottom Arm Motion

The bottom arm begins the force phase by pulling downward a few inches into the water. At the end of the catch, the elbow bends and the hand turns, palm facing toward the feet. With the fingers relaxed and slightly spread, the hand continues to pull under the body and parallel to it. The force phase continues until the hand is beneath the shoulder.

The recovery phase starts with the hand and elbow underneath the shoulder. The flexed arm collapses into the side of the body. The hand moves in toward the ear and turns as the arm begins to extend back to its starting position. The arm remains straight throughout the glide.

Top Arm Motion

The top arm begins its recovery in a manner identical to the lift of the arm in the crawl stroke recovery. The arm comes out of the water with the elbow leading and the wrist higher than the hand. The arm extends to a position near the chin for entry. The fingers are slightly spread and the wrist is relaxed. It is not uncommon to have the top hand pass over the bottom hand as the hands meet in front of the chin. Some students visualize the act of picking an apple (with the bottom arm) and putting it in a basket (the top arm) as it turns to push.

The thrust of the force phase of the top arm comes when the hand, palm facing backward, pushes the water back toward the feet. The hand makes a path straight back along the body line ending on top of the thigh.

Scissors Kick

The scissors kick is the same one used in the basic sidestroke. Refer to Chapter Seven for details concerning the proper technique for the kick.

Breathing Cycle and Coordination of the Stroke

The breathing cycle is not significant since the face is out of the water. Breathing should be as natural as possible.

The coordination of the overarm sidestroke is similar to the basic sidestroke with one or two exceptions. Begin by pulling with the bottom arm (force phase). Near the end of the pull, the other three limbs begin recovering. It may be wise to delay the recovery movement of the legs slightly.

It takes longer to execute an overarm motion than an underwater one, thus the legs should not flex until the top arm touches the water. As the top arm slices into the water and positions the hand for the forceful pull, the legs should be in position to exert force. While the legs and the top arm drive the body through the water, the bottom arm is extended straight up from the shoulder. The head rests on the upper arm to create the least water resistance. The force phase of the top arm and legs is followed by a short glide. When body momentum begins to subside, the stroke begins again.

TROUBLESHOOTING THE OVERARM SIDESTROKE

STROKE DEFICIENCY   SOLUTION

Body position and scissors kick is covered under sidestroke.

Top Arm Motion

STROKE DEFICIENCY	SOLUTION
Hand moves too far forward during recovery causing the body to roll on the front.	Enter hand near chin instead of further extension as in the front crawl.
Stopping the top arm during force phase at the waist and losing power.	Press with the top arm through to the thigh as in the front crawl.
Recovering arm underwater away from the body will cause negative water resistance.	Lift elbow high to recover arm.

TRUDGEN CRAWL STROKE

In the late 1800's a man named John Trudgen of England invented a stroke with the arm movement of the crawl and a scissors kick. This stroke became known as the *Trudgen*. Today it is called the Single Trudgen. In the 1960's and early 1970's, swimming instructors in the United States were teaching three different types of trudgen stroke, the Single Trudgen, the Double Trudgen and the Trudgen Crawl. Although all three versions of the stroke use an alternating over the water arm movement and a scissors kick, the Trudgen Crawl includes a three-beat flutter kick.

The Single Trudgen uses one scissors kick at the moment a bite of air is taken. As the arm on the breathing side pulls through the water, the legs remain relaxed and inactive. Force is created by the legs only during every other arm pull. This produces an uneven stroke with a glide or hesitation on one side. The only redeeming feature of the stroke is that it can be used by crawl stroke swimmers whose legs become tired after flutter kicking for some time. Some older swimmers prefer this stroke because they can swim greater distances with ease while using it.

The Double Trudgen uses two scissors kicks. One scissors kick on the breathing side and one on the non-breathing side. Difficulty may be experienced while executing a scissors kick on the non-breathing side since the body rotation is less than on the breathing side. The stroke has two short glides at the end of each scissors kick while the arms stop their action momentarily. This produces a very awkward looking stroke with marked hesitations and loss of speed.

The Trudgen Crawl is the most difficult of the three versions to execute. It uses a crawl stroke arm movement while alternately combining a scissors kick and three flutter kicks for the leg movement. Because of the two different kicks used in each stroke, it is perhaps the most challenging of the three trudgens to learn. Only this variation of the trudgen will be fully discussed in this chapter.

Starting Body Position and Arm Motion

The body is in a prone position. The starting form is the same as for the front crawl. The arm motions are identical to those of the front crawl. For a description of these skills see Chapter Seven.

Trudgen Crawl Kick

The original trudgen stroke used the arm motions of the front crawl and the scissors kick. That is why the trudgen kick is commonly thought to be a scissors kick. The single and double trudgens use only scissor kicks.

The kick in the crawl stroke is commonly called a flutter or crawl kick. The name "trudgen-crawl kick" denotes that both a scissors kick and a flutter kick are included. Both kicks have been thoroughly described in Chapter Seven.

In this stroke the scissors kick and flutter kick are used alternately. The scissors kick used in the trudgen crawl is narrower than that used in the sidestroke. It is combined with three flutter kicks. Thus one scissors and three flutter kicks occur during each stroke cycle.

Breathing Cycle and Coordination of Stroke

The breathing cycle is the same as for the front crawl stroke. The head is in the water to the hairline and the face turns to the breathing side to take a bite of air. The head returns to a face-down position in the water for exhalation as soon as the hand passes the face on its way to a water entry. The cycle continues.

Generally, the stroke can be described as performing a narrowed scissors kick on the breathing side and three flutter kicks on the non-breathing side while the face is in the water.

Specifically, the arm on the breathing side pulls through to the hip, while the legs execute three flutter kicks. As the arm on the non-breathing side begins the force phase, the body is rolled slightly toward the breathing side and the legs are drawn up with the heels behind the buttocks. The scissors kick is executed as the arm on the non-breathing side pulls the body forward. At this time a breath is taken and the arm on the breathing side begins the recovery phase.

TROUBLESHOOTING THE TRUDGEN-CRAWL STROKE

STROKE DEFICIENCY	SOLUTION
Body Position	
Head is too high forcing hips and legs down.	Head should be at hairline level as in the front crawl.

Arm motions are the same as in the Front Crawl.

Leg Motions	
Bending too much at the knees on the downbeat, forces water downward instead of backward.	Deliver three flutter kicks in normal fashion as one arm pulls.

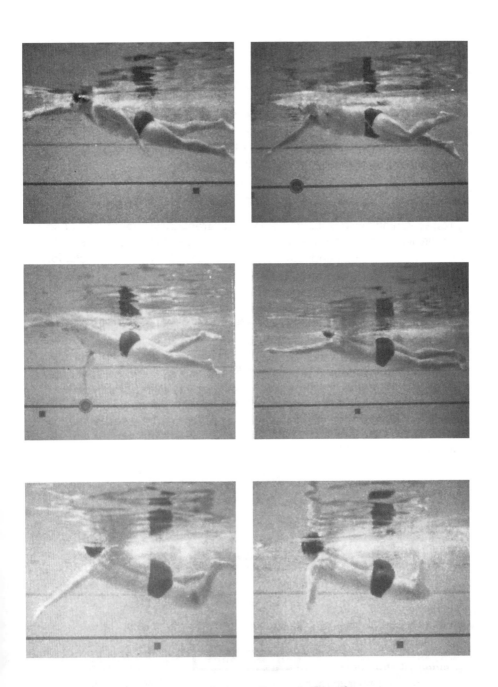

The Trudgen Crawl Stroke

Tendency to deliver wide flutter kick and not a scissors.	Deliver a single scissors kick while other arm is pulling.

Breathing Cycle and Coordination of Stroke

Forgetting to inhale and exhale properly causes an exhausting stroke.	Use firmly established cycle of breathing as in the front crawl.
Executing too many flutter kicks causes loss of stroke mechanics.	Perform three flutter kicks as the arm on the breathing side pulls.

INVERTED BREASTSTROKE

The inverted breaststroke is a combination of the arm stroke of the breaststroke in a face-up position and the whip kick of the elementary backstroke (supine position). It can be a very relaxed stroke to swim on the back, especially if the swimmer has good buoyancy and can maintain a straight body position in the water. The sequencing of the stroke parallels that of the basic breaststroke. The arms pull, the legs kick, and the stroke ends in an abbreviated glide. All movements are performed beneath the surface of the water as in the elementary backstroke.

Starting Body Position

The body starts in a back-lying position in the water. The arms are extended over head with the thumbs about six inches apart and the palms facing upward. The legs are extended with the feet together. The hips are high, a few inches from the surface. The back of the head is submerged to approximately ear level.

Arm Motion

The palms are turned toward the feet at the beginning of the force phase. The arms press against the water until they come into contact with the sides. A slight bend in the elbows is acceptable during the force phase. The palms of the hands come in contact with the sides of the thighs to complete the thrust portion of the stroke.

The recovery of the arms begins immediately. The hands are drawn up the sides of the body with the thumbs leading. The elbows should remain pointed down toward the bottom of the pool to limit resistance, just as in the elementary backstroke. When the hands are just below the armpits, the palms rotate to an upward position as the hands slide over the shoulder joint. As the arms continue extending upward, the palms slip under the ears, the elbows face sideways. The arms fully extend to finish the recovery phase.

The glide occurs when the arms return to the starting position. The body is straight and streamlined to cut through the water. When momentum ceases, the arms begin the force phase and the stroke is repeated.

Whip Kick

The whip kick used in the elementary backstroke is the same one executed in the inverted breaststroke. The mechanics of the kick were described in Chapter Seven.

The important part played by this kick should not be underestimated. The timing of the whip kick in this stroke is crucial to the successful performance of the stroke.

Coordination of the Stroke

It is probably safe to say that the arms complete the force phase and half of the recovery phase before the legs perform the whip kick. The legs remain straight until the arms reach a position with the hands touching the armpits during the recovery phase. As the hands turn palms upward and slide over the shoulders, the legs begin to recover. The lower legs from knee to ankle drop down, and the toes of both feet turn outward with the heels facing each other. With the hands under the ears, poised for a quick extension, the legs execute the whip. At the same time the arms fully extend into the glide or starting position. A short glide concludes the stroke, then the arms begin their pull to initiate another stroke.

Breathing Cycle

Since the stroke is performed in a supine position with the face out of the water the entire time, the breathing cycle does not seem to be a problem for most swimmers. It is generally suggested that the swimmer inhale during the recovery of the arms with the chin slightly elevated. During the force phase of the arms and legs the swimmer should drop the chin slightly in order to facilitate exhalation. This will allow him to look down the body and get a better sense of direction for swimming in a straight line or parallel to the side of the pool.

The chin-up, chin-down technique can also be used for the elementary backstroke. It is not uncommon for a beginner to recover the hands too high and push water into his face, making breathing difficult.

TROUBLESHOOTING THE INVERTED BREASTSTROKE

STROKE DEFICIENCY **SOLUTION**

Body Position

Tendency to sit in the water retards forward motion.	Stretch arms overhead, legs stretch out, streamline body.

Arm Motions

Recovering arms hastily may stop forward momentum.	Carefully recovery arms under head and stretch out on glide.
Letting the arms come out of the water on recovery forces the rest of the body down.	The upper body drops down when the arms are too far out of the water.
Not straightening the arms out for the glide creates water resistance.	Recover arms straight up from the hips to a position straight overhead with a break in continuity.
Shortening the force phase by stopping halfway causes loss of propulsion.	Press arms through to the thighs before completing the force phase.

Whip Kick

See the Elementary Backstroke for faults and corrections.

Coordination of Stroke

Eliminating the glide causes coordination problems.	Execute a glide for a few moments before starting the arm press.
Recovering the legs too early may result in loss of propulsion.	Prepare the legs for kicking as the hands pass the shoulders on the way forward during the recovery.

THE BUTTERFLY STROKE

This stroke was first performed with the breaststroke kick. It was the middle of the 20th century before the dolphin kick was adopted as the official kick to be used in the butterfly. In 1952 the stroke was accepted as a competitive stroke. The butterfly is not a variation of other strokes. Both the overarm motions and the dolphin kick are different than the arm and leg movements used in the basic strokes.

Although the butterfly is a beautiful stroke to watch in competitive meets, it is not commonly used in recreational swimming. It is presented here for the experienced swimmer who would like to accept the challenge and learn this powerful stroke.

Starting Body Position

The body begins in a front-lying position with the face in the water, arms extended overhead and close together. The legs are fully extended and the feet are together. The knees may be slightly bent in preparation for the dolphin kick which begins the stroke. The feet are usually relaxed and pigeon-toed. The head is submerged deeper in the water at the beginning of the stroke than it is in any of the other strokes.

Dolphin Kick

The dolphin kick is the fastest of all kicks when performed alone or on a kick board. The kick is difficult for some swimmers because it requires a great deal of ankle and hip flexibility. The dolphin kick can be generally described as two flutter kicks in a row using both legs at the same time. It has also been called the fishtail kick.

As the kick begins, both legs bend at the knees and the legs separate slightly. The ankles are extended and the toes are pointed. Both legs whip downward to a depth of approximately two feet. The legs are fully extended at the completion of the downward kick. The feet also assist in the whipping action. This first kick is usually the most vigorous of the two kicks.

At the end of the downward beat, the hips are lifted and assist the body to prepare for the second kick. The function of the second kick is to cancel the hip-dropping effect of the latter part of the pull. The forcefulness of the latter part of the arm pull may produce a second kick as strong as the first. But this can only be performed for a short time because of its strenuous nature.

At the end of the first kick, the legs are brought up to the surface with no bend in the knees. The lifting of the legs causes the hips to drops. The knees then bend forming an angle of approximately 90 degrees. The feet point toward the surface of the water prior to the force phase.

The feet thrust downward, with the legs fully extended at the end of the second downward thrust. The upper part of the legs move toward the surface. At this point, the dolphin kick is completed and the cycle begins again.

Arm Motion

The arm action of the butterfly stroke has been generally described as a key hole, hour glass, or double "S" pull. In other words, the hands enter the water apart, then swing in and under the body for the press, and come out around the hips and up for the recovery. This is called an "out-in-out" movement.

The arms enter the water in much the same way as they do in the front crawl. The elbows are high, with the wrist higher than the hand as the fingers reach forward for the entry above the head on a line straight out from the shoulder joint. If the swimmer thinks of reaching over a barrel, the elbows will stay high, placing the arms in a good position to push the water backward effectively. The palms face outward as the arms bend to almost 90 degrees and begin the outward, backward and downward thrust. After pulling past the shoulders, the hands come in under the body for the push toward the feet. The force phase is completed as the hands come out of the water in the hip region, just as in the front crawl.

The arm recovery begins as the hands leave the water in a palm-up position, the elbows are slightly bent. The arms swing forward in a low, flat trajectory. They completely extend due largely to the centrifugal force produced by their circular motion. The arm muscles contract vigorously during the first part of the arm swing, then relax and allow the momentum to carry them forward. The hands enter the water at a point just outside the shoulder line, with the palms facing downward and slightly outward. The thumbs should be lower than the rest of the hands.

Butterfly underwater stroke pattern

Breathing Cycle

A breath is taken as the arms begin the recovery and swing forward for the water entry. As the arms enter the water, the neck muscles should relax and the head should drop down until it is in alignment with the body. Swimmers who are learning the stroke should breathe during every arm cycle. Competitive swimmers usually breathe once every two cycles.

Coordination of the Stroke

The stroke cycle begins with the arms entering the water at shoulder width. The legs are ready to begin the downward thrust of the kick. The head is tilted forward. As the arms pull diagonally outward, the feet press downward. The pull causes the head to come up, but it does not come out of the water. It is best to look forward with the eyes open.

As the arms reach their maximum spread, the legs have completed the first leg kick and are recovering to begin the second. The arms start to come together, almost touching as they pass under the shoulders. The elbow flexion at this point is about 90 degrees. The elbows then collapse into the body as the hands pass under the shoulders. The downward thrust of the second kick begins as the hands start upward during the last part of the pull. The head drops slightly as the arms start to swing out and upward for the recovery.

The legs complete the downward thrust just before the hands leave the water. As the hands come up out of the water, the legs come straight up toward the top of the water. The head is lowered so that the face is directly downward. This allows greater efficiency for the arm recovery phase. As the hands swing forward, the palms face downward and the elbows are completely extended. The feet begin to point toward the surface, and the knee flexion increases in preparation for the first downbeat of the first kick. Then the cycle begins again.

TROUBLESHOOTING THE BUTTERFLY STROKE

STROKE DEFICIENCY   SOLUTION

Body Position

| A sharp pike position may retard forward progress. | Minimize hip lift and downward press of kick. |

Arm Actions

| Hands entering the water too wide limit the force of propulsion. | Enter water just outside shoulder width for best results. |

Straight arms on force phase sacrifices power.

Use a bent arm, drive out and in for the first part of the force phase.

Dropping the elbows during the force phase causes the body to move upward rather than forward.

Keep elbows up until the press toward the feet is complete.

Stopping the arm action at the point of entry causes the body to bob up and down.

Keep the momentum going from the arm recovery motion to carry the arms down to a ten inch depth before pulling.

Dolphin Kick

Lack of full extension of knees during downbeat can result in loss of power.

Press feet downward and use knees to whip lower legs to full extension.

Failing to bring the legs up straight will cause the hips to stay too high for proper undulation.

The upbeat of the kick must have a straight leg position for the major part of the recovery phase.

A narrow kick prevents the arms from recovering correctly not allowing enough breathing time.

Increase the width of the kick to about two feet.

Breathing Cycle and Coordination of Stroke

Raising the head too high to breathe slows forward propulsion.

Raise head only to lower lip, jut chin out to catch breath.

Stopping the force phase of the arms short of the hips interferes with the second kick.

Remember to bring arms all the way through to hips before exiting the water.

Delaying the timing of the downstrokes of the kicks make coordination difficult.

Begin to kick down first at arm entry, and the second kick down with arm force phase.

Slow downbeats of kicks reduces speed of stroke.

Kick downward faster than upward on the dolphin kicks.

The Butterfly Stroke

SUMMARY

The accomplished swimmer should be able to perform the basic swimming strokes at a high level of efficiency. He should also be thoroughly familiar with the strokes that are frequently referred to as advanced strokes. These include the overarm sidestroke, trudgen crawl, inverted breaststroke and butterfly stroke.

Although most of the "advanced strokes" are not difficult, they offer a challenge. The swimmer must either change a part of a stroke previously learned or change the coordination or change both. The butterfly stroke is the most difficult of these strokes. It involves a new kick as well as a double over water recovery of the arms.

REVIEW QUESTIONS

1. In what ways does the overarm sidestroke differ from the conventional sidestroke?
2. How does the coordination of the inverted breaststroke differ from the elementary backstroke?
3. How is the scissors kick modified in the trudgen crawl? Why is this necessary?
4. Why is the butterfly a very tiring stroke to swim?
5. What would be the main purpose for using each of the advanced strokes?

SELECTED REFERENCES

1. American National Red Cross. (1981). *Swimming and Aquatics Safety.* Washington, DC: American National Red Cross.
2. Bland, H., (1979). *Competitive Swimming.* England: E. P. Publishing Ltd.
3. Gaughran, J.A., (1972). *Advanced Swimming.* Dubuque, IA: Wm. C. Brown.
4. Maglischo, E.W., (1982). *Swimming Faster.* Palo Alto, CA: Mayfield.
5. Midtlyng, J., (1982). *Swimming.* (2nd Ed.), Philadelphia, PA: W. B. Saunders.
6. Vickers, B. J. & Vincent, W. J., (1984). *Swimming.* (4th Ed.), Dubuque, IA: Wm. C. Brown.

CHAPTER 10
Diving Basics

Soon after learning to swim, many individuals express a desire to learn how to dive. For some, this means a simple head-first entry from the side of the pool. For others, diving means the ability to enter the water by using a forward dive with an approach from a one meter diving board. Other students may have a goal to learn a wide variety of forward and backward dives from the one meter board.

In this chapter, discussion will be limited to diving from the edge of the pool and to a forward dive from a one meter board using a three step approach with a hurdle. Students who wish to go beyond this level should enroll in a diving class or seek private lessons from an experienced diving teacher or coach.

SAFETY IN DIVING

Each year hundreds of individuals experience serious injuries in diving accidents. Many of these lead to injuries that cause permanent paralysis. (Motor cycle accidents and diving accidents are leading causes of injuries that result in paralysis.) In order to prevent the possibility of such an accident, certain safety rules must be kept in mind when considering a headfirst entry into a body of water. These rules are discussed below.

RULE: *Never dive into a body of water until you have tested it by entering feet first.*

A sign currently being used in some pools reads: "Feet First, First Time".

When approaching a body of water for the first time, it is important for the swimmer to become familiar with the depth and the slope of the bottom. A feet first entry will prevent the possibility of diving into water that is too shallow for a safe dive.

RULE: Never make a head first entry into water that is less than five feet deep.

Most diving accidents occur in water that is less than five feet deep. An individual who makes a small miscalculation in his angle of take-off could easily strike his head in shallow water.

RULE: Never dive off a pier unless the area is marked for diving.

A number of serious accidents have occurred in areas where water depth changes. This could be due to tides, shifting sands on the bottom, or even draught conditions that have reduced water depth. There is always a possibility that water is more shallow than expected.

RULE: In a pool, dive straight off the end of the board.

An individual who dives toward the side of the pool may strike his head on the pool wall.

RULE: In a pool, do not attempt to dive out as far as possible.

In most pools, the bottom is deepest directly below and a few feet in front of the diving board. Pools slope upward at various distances in front of the board. Individuals who dive out too far, risk the possibility of striking their heads on the slope.

RULE: Look before jumping or diving from the side or from the diving board.

It is the diver's responsibility to make sure that no one is in the water near the point of entry. By checking the area before diving, he will avoid injuring himself as well as another person.

APPLICATION OF SELECTED PHYSICAL LAWS TO DIVING

The *Law of Inertia* (Newton's First Law) states that a force must be exerted to put an object in motion, to change its direction or to stop its motion. In other words, Inertia (the resistance to change) must be overcome in order to move the body either in a standing dive or in a dive from an approach.

Muscular force is used to overcome inertia in order to get the body moving as well as to change direction. In a springboard dive, a directional change occurs when the diver moves from the last step into the hurdle. At this point he changes his forward momentum to upward momentum.

One important principle that is related to Newton's Second Law (the *Law of Acceleration*) states that shortening a lever increases angular velocity and lengthening the lever decreases angular velocity, if the force remains constant. In diving this principle can easily be demonstrated. A dive can be done in one of three positions: tuck, pike or layout. If a dive is done in layout position, the body will rotate from a head up to a head down position fairly slowly. If the same dive is done in tuck position, the body will rotate much quicker. The diver can increase the speed of rotation by tucking tighter.

The Law of Reaction (Newton's Third Law) states that for every action there is an equal and opposite reaction. In a standing dive this law comes into play as the diver uses the muscles of the lower limbs to push downward and backward against the supporting surface. The supporting surface will push against the feet of the diver with an equal amount of force, but in the opposite direction causing the diver to move in a forward, upward direction.

On the diving board, the diver must also be aware of the Law of Reaction since it comes into play frequently. One example would be a situation in which the diver drops his head on his descent. This causes his legs to rotate past the desired near vertical position for entry. This law also comes into play when the arms are thrown to the left. This will cause the hips to twist to the right.

The principle of *Transfer of Momentum* states that momentum that is developed in a segment of the body may be transferred to the whole body while the body is in contact with a supporting surface. In both the standing dive and the dive with an approach, the arms swing forward and upward. This swinging action creates momentum in the arms which is transferred to the entire body. The diver will get either greater height or greater distance in his dive depending on the directional thrust of the arms (upward = greater height, forward = greater distance).

Time in Flight is another important principle for the diver. The length of time that an object remains in the air is dependent upon its maximum height. In springboard diving, maximum height must be attained in order for the diver to have enough time to complete his maneuvers in good form.

ELEMENTARY HEAD FIRST ENTRIES

The student should practice each of the steps in the learning sequence described in this section. He should be sure to master each of the following Key Factors as he practices each successive step.

✓ Keep the eyes focused on the point of entry.

✓ Stretch the arms out overhead with the upper arms pressed tightly against the ears.

✓ Hold the entry position as the body sinks below the surface of the water.

When the student has experienced success and has become comfortable with the step that he is practicing, he is ready to move on to the next step.

Sitting Dive

The sitting dive is an easy technique which is used to help the student overcome any fear that he may have of entering the water head first. It is usually considered to be the first step in learning to dive.

To perform the sitting dive, start by sitting on the edge of the pool with the legs in the water. Spread the knees wide apart and rest the soles of the feet in the gutter or against the side of the pool. Stretch the arms overhead with the upper arms pressed against the ears. Drop the head so that the chin touches the sternum. Take a deep breath and focus the eyes on the water below. Roll forward, reach for the water with the hands and push against the wall with the feet. While rolling forward, the hands should be aimed at an imaginary target below the surface of the water. Be sure that the hands do not "slip off target" as forward movement continues. Hold the position as the body enters the water. Once the body is completely in the water, the student should lift his head and return to the surface. To prevent water from going up the nose, blow air out through the nostrils.

Kneeling Dive

The second step in the learning sequence for the forward dive is the kneeling dive. This technique will give the student more of a feel for the dive. Since he is slightly higher off the surface of the water, he will have to experience falling further before he enters the water.

Kneel at the edge of the pool with the right knee down and the toes of the right foot curled under. (Leg and foot positions may be reversed.) The toes of the left foot should be curled over the edge of the pool to prevent the foot from slipping. Stretch the arms overhead with the upper arms pressed against the ears. Select a target three to four feet from the edge of the pool. Drop the head as in the sitting dive. Aim the hands at the target and focus the eyes on the water below.

Begin to lean forward. As the body begins to fall, push down and back against the deck with the left foot. Straighten the left knee and lift the right leg into the air to help drive the body down into the water. Bring the left leg up beside the right leg so that the legs enter the water together. Hold the position until the body is completely under water. Then lift the head to help the body change direction and come back to the surface.

One Legged Dive

If the kneeling dive was done correctly, this step will be fairly easy. The weight of one leg above the head is used to help the body move quickly and easily down into the water. Diving deep at this point will help the student enter the water without landing flat. A shallow dive can easily be learned once the student has mastered the techniques needed to dive deep.

Stand at the edge of the pool with one leg forward and one back. Wrap the toes of the forward foot over the edge of the pool deck. Keep the knees of both legs straight and the weight over the forward foot.

Stretch the arms up overhead while squeezing the ears with the upper arms. Drop the chin and bend forward at the waist. Aim the hands at a point three to four feet from the side of the pool. Keeping both knees straight, lift the back leg high in the air as the upper body continues to bend forward. As the body falls toward the water, bring the forward leg up so that the legs are together as they enter the water. Hold the position until the body is under water. Then lift the head to return to the surface.

Two Legged Dive

Because of the change in the starting position and the necessity to produce a strong pushing action with the feet and legs, this step in the diving sequence may be difficult for some students. Students should develop confidence in their ability to perform the one legged dive prior to attempting the two legged dive. Once this step has been mastered the student will be ready to work on either a long shallow dive or a dive from the edge of the pool with a spring.

Start in an erect standing position with the toes of both feet curled over the edge of the deck. Squeeze the ears with the upper arms as the arms are stretched high overhead.

Begin with a slight lean to cause the center of gravity to move forward past the feet. Then bend the knees slightly. Quickly straighten the knees and forcefully extend the ankles. This action should give the body a little springing action. The diver should reach for the water with the hands after the take-off. However, the arms, head and shoulders should stay aligned with the body. Hold the position as the body enters the water. Return to the surface.

Beginning Diving Learning Sequence

STANDING DIVE WITH SPRING

Once the basic dive has been learned, it should be easy for the student to make the necessary adjustments to add a spring to a dive from the edge of the pool. To accomplish this the student must use the arms to get additional lift in order to pull the body up into the air in a springing action.

Arm Action

Start with the arms extended to the sides at shoulder level. Drop the arms to the sides. Bend the elbows to bring the hands to the shoulders. Forcefully extend the arms straight upward above the shoulders. This set of movements must be continuous from start to finish.

Coordination of Arms and Legs

Stand erect with the arms extended at shoulder level, the feet together and the toes wrapped over the edge of the deck. As the arms drop to the sides and the elbows bend, flex the hips and knees. Extend the arms forcefully overhead. At the same time lean forward slightly and use the feet and legs to push downward and backward against the deck. Finish the arm extension with the arms stretched overhead and the upper arms pressing against the ears. Try to get the feeling of diving over a barrel. Look for the water. Keep the feet together and the toes pointed. Continue to stretch until the feet enter the water.

> HINT: Students who have difficulty getting spring in their dives should try diving over a pole. Have a partner hold the pole at knee level eight to ten inches in front of the legs. Dive over the pole. The partner should drop the pole, if it appears as though the diver may hit it.

SHALLOW DIVE

At times a swimmer may want to use a dive to get into the water quickly without going deep. In those instances, the shallow dive would be appropriate. The shallow dive is used in recreational swimming and lifesaving.

Start with the feet shoulder width apart and the toes curled over the edge of the deck. The hips and knees should be flexed. The head should be up to enable the diver to focus on the point of entry. The arms should hang straight down beneath the shoulders.

Begin by drawing the arms backward and upward. The body should begin leaning forward. Without hesitation, the arms change direction and swing downward and forward. The hips, knees and ankles extend to exert a backward thrust against the edge of the deck. The head drops and the outstretched arms hug the ears. The legs come together and the toes point to help streamline the body. The body should enter the water at a low angle. Glide until momentum is lost, then begin stroking.

SPRINGBOARD DIVING

Modern diving boards have been designed to allow the diver to get a great deal of spring. It is this spring that enables the diver to have enough flight time to perform his maneuvers. With practice anyone can learn to effectively use the available spring to improve his diving technique.

The Fulcrum

The fulcrum is a point of support for the diving board, around which the board can flex. Diving boards which have been installed in most competitive pools have moveable fulcrums. This allows the diver to actually change the length of the portion of the board that will flex. By moving the fulcrum back, the board will have a greater amount of spring. Moving the fulcrum forward will reduce the amount of spring. Beginning divers should move the fulcrum as far forward as possible.

Steps to Learning the Dive

Just as in the dive from the side of the pool, it is necessary to progress through a series of steps to learn to dive from a board. Follow the steps as described below to learn a simple forward dive with a three step approach and a hurdle.

Step 1: Fall-in Dive

The fall-in dive is used to help the beginning diver become accustomed to entering from a greater height above the water. It is also used to practice the proper entry. Do not attempt to get any spring while practicing the fall in dive.

Stand erect on the end of the diving board with the feet together and the toes wrapped around the edge. Raise the arms sideward to shoulder level. Keep the arms out to the side and the legs straight while bending forward at the hips. Look at the water throughout the dive. Lean forward.

As the body falls toward the water, raise the arms up overhead with the hands together and the upper arms pressing the ears. Stretch toward the water, keep the feet together and the toes pointed. Hold the position until the feet enter the water.

Step 2: Standing Dive

The standing dive from the end of the board allows the student to get the feel for a small amount of spring from the board. It also gives the student the opportunity to practice controlling his flight and entry from a greater height off the surface of the water.

This technique is identical to the standing dive with spring from the side of the pool. Review the description of this technique on page 121 and then practice it from the end of the diving board. Be sure to look at the water to prevent the legs from rotating too far.

Step 3: Approach

The approach for the forward dive from the board consists of three steps, plus a hurdle step (a spring from one foot near the end of the board) and a two-foot take-off. This same approach is used for all forward dives, all reverse dives and some twisting dives. Therefore, learning the proper approach is a very important step in learning to dive.

First it is necessary to determine the proper starting point on the board for the approach. This is done in the following manner. Walk to the end of the board, turn around and line the heels up with the end of the board. Take four normal walking steps and turn around. This should be the approximate starting position for the approach.

It is also necessary to determine on which foot the first step should be taken. Using a three step approach plus a hurdle, the take-off for the hurdle will be on the same foot on which the first step is taken. One way to determine which foot to start with is to kick a ball. The foot that is used to kick a ball is probably the foot to use for the hurdle take-off. Therefore, it is the foot with which to take the first step.

Stand erect on the board at the point which was determined to be the proper starting position. With the head erect, focus the eyes on the end of the board. Take three normal walking steps at medium speed. Allow the arms to hang at the sides without swinging during the first two steps. During the last step draw the arms backward to a point six to eight inches behind the hips.

Both arms begin to swing forward and then upward as the body moves over the hurdle leg and the knee begins to bend in preparation for the hurdle. The other leg is brought forward and upward with a bent knee as the arms continue upward to an overhead position. This helps to lift the body.

The take-off leg extends at the hip, knee and ankle joints to push down against the board. The other leg continues upward until the thigh is in a horizontal position with the knee bent at a 90 degree angle. The take-off leg remains extended and the other leg extends with the feet together and the toes pointed. The arms drop from a position of extension overhead to a point just above the shoulders.

The diver lands on the balls of both feet. The feet should be eight to ten inches apart for balance. At the same time the arms are brought down and back and then up in a circular pattern. The heels are lowered onto the board as the knees, hips and ankles flex. At this point the diver should focus his eyes on the water in front of the board with his head up. Next the arms reach up as the knees, hips and ankles extend and the body is hurled into the air.

Practice the approach with a jump into the air. Keep the back straight, head up, feet together and toes pointed. Drop the arms from the overhead position to a position along the sides of the body after leaving the board.

Step 4: Approach and Dive

The diver should follow the procedures described for performing the three step approach and hurdle. At the end of the approach and hurdle the diver leans forward slightly as he leaves the board. The legs come together with the toes pointed as in the jump. Upon reaching the maximum height from the take-off, the diver drops his head forward and sets the arms by dropping them sideward to facilitate forward rotation of the body. The body remains extended and the eyes focus on the point of entry. He stretches the arms back over the head and holds his position until his feet enter the water.

The Springboard Dive

The Springboard Dive cont.

The Springboard Dive cont.

SUMMARY

Diving is an important skill for those who engage in swimming activities. It is used in recreational swimming as well as in the process of making a rescue in lifesaving. Those who engage in diving activities should be well aware of the safety rules as they relate to entering the water head first.

By following a logical series of steps, the beginner can become proficient in diving from the edge of the pool. Once he has developed the basics of diving from the edge of the pool, he is ready to learn a simple dive with a three step approach and hurdle from the one meter diving board. After mastering this simple dive, the student may want to learn the forward dive in layout or pike position or go on to the back dive.

REVIEW QUESTIONS

1. Give an example of the application of the Law of Inertia to diving from the board.

2. What would be the most important rule to follow in terms of safety in diving? Explain.

3. Why are the arms used during the hurdle in the dive from the board? Explain in relation to the laws of motion.

4. Why should the diver hold his position until his feet enter the water?

5. In doing the standing dive from the edge of the pool, why should the diver use the upper arms to squeeze the ears?

SELECTED REFERENCES

1. Miller, D. I., (1984). *Biomechanical Characteristics of the Final Approach, Step, Hurdle, and Takeoff of Elite American Springboard Divers*. Journal of Human Movement Studies. 10, 189-212.

2. Miller, D. I. & Munro, C. F., (1984). *Body Contribution to Height Achieved During the Flight of a Springboard Dive*. Medicine and Science in Sports and Exercise. 16 (3)), 234-242.

3. Miller, D. I. & Munro, C. F., (1985a). *Greg Louganis' Springboard Takeoff* I. *Temporal and Joint Position Analysis*. International Journal of Sport Biomechanics. 1, 209-220.

4. Miller, D. I. & Munro, C. F., (1985b). *Greg Louganis' Springboard Takeoff* II. *Linear and Angular Momentum Considerations*. International Journal of Sport Biomechanics. 1, 288-307.

5. Sanders, R. H. & Wilson, B. D., (1988). *Factors Contributing to Maximum Height of Dives after Takeoff from the 3M Springboard*. International Journal of Sport Biomechanics. 4 (3), 231-259.

CHAPTER 11
Personal Survival and Rescue Skills

Rarely is the possibility of a near drowning experience considered when planning a day at the beach or pool. However, the chance of becoming involved in an emergency situation is always present. Those who engage in aquatic activities should take the time to learn and practice both personal survival and rescue skills. Advance preparation may avert panic as well as prevent a disaster.

Unexpected personal emergencies that may be encountered by a swimmer include: muscle cramps, currents, undertows, and weeds. The swimmer may also find a need for knowledge and skills related to small craft safety, rescue and search procedures, disrobing, rescue breathing, and back and neck injuries. These and other skills related to personal survival and rescue skills will be discussed in this chapter.

MUSCLE CRAMPS

Muscle cramps usually happen without warning causing extreme pain in the calf of the leg, foot, toes, fingers or hand. Although abdominal cramps are possible, they are extremely rare. The affected part contracts into a tight knot inhibiting further motion. Do not panic. Stretch or extend the muscle or knead it with the hands.

In case of a muscle cramp in the calf of the leg, bend down as in a jellyfish float position and begin to vigorously knead the belly of the muscle. Come up for a breath and repeat the process, continuing to massage until relief comes. If the shore, pier or pool deck is near, move to safety. Then stretch the calf muscle by grabbing the foot and pulling it toward the shin. For a cramp in the hand, knead the affected muscle while treading water. In case of cramps in the foot, use the jellyfish float position while massaging the affected area.

To prevent cramps avoid fatigue, cold, or overexertion. At the first sign of a problem, change strokes or attempt to stretch the affected muscle. This may avert a cramp or cause sufficient relief to get back to safety.

CURRENTS AND UNDERTOWS

River currents often carry unwary swimmers dangerously far from shore. These intense underwater channels vary according to the volume of water and the depth of the riverbed. Large rocks, fallen trees, backwaters, islands, and the contour of the river all contribute to the treacherous nature of underwater currents.

Ocean currents are caused by the action of large waves upon the shoreline. The water level rises and causes the "tide" current to come in. This creates the "ebb" current as the water recedes. Tides can come in with great force causing problems for swimmers.

Undertows, also called a "backwash", are caused by the action of water rushing down the beach back under the oncoming waves. The force of the undertow may knock a person off his feet and drag him under the water. Currents and undertows are also affected by changes in weather conditions. The swimmer should be wary of the effects of environmental changes.

The main principle for swimmers to remember is, never swim **against**, but always diagonally **across** a current. Even the best swimmer cannot withstand most river and ocean currents. It may be necessary to swim some distance to become free and return to shore.

UNDERWATER WEEDS

Underwater weeds, and long grass can cause the unsuspecting swimmer to become entangled and subsequently panic. Sudden twisting and turning may worsen the situation. Slowly and gently shake the weeds loose and withdraw the limbs. A water weed called "kelp" may form a thick bed on top of the water. when swimming underwater, the swimmer may come to the surface underneath kelp. Do not attempt to go through it. Part the weeds, come up for a breath, then dive under the weeds and come up in a clear area.

ELEMENTARY FORMS OF RESCUE
Reaching Assists

In a situation in which a swimmer is in trouble, the first instinct of those nearby is to reach out with a hand, leg, or towel. Whether on a pier or pool deck or in neck deep water, stabilization of the body is absolutely necessary before a reaching rescue is attempted. the proper position is lying flat on the pier or pool deck with the body anchored to something or someone. Lean back or hold onto another person, if standing in neck deep water. When reaching out to make the rescue, let the victim grab your hand, leg, or end of a towel. It may be necessary to grab the victim by the hair, arm, or some other body part in an effort to bring the person to the surface. If possible, grasp the wrist and slowly pull the victim to safety, keeping his head above water at all times. If the victim is conscious, continually and calmly reassure him as the rescue is made.

When the victim is too far away to be reached with an arm, leg or towel; the rescuer should quickly find an object that can be used to extend his reach. Clothing items that can be useful for extension include: a belt, long sleeved shirt, or a jacket. On a pier the rescuer may find a fishing pole, canoe paddle, or boat oar. On shore, look for a tree branch or floating device with a rope attached. A spare tire or tube is also buoyant and can be pushed out to rescue a conscious victim.

Reaching assist with a pole

Reaching assist with a towel or clothing

Wading Rescues

If a victim falls into a drop-off, the rescuer should wade out into the water to within reach of the victim. The rescuer should grab the victim and pull him to safety. To safely perform this technique, the rescuer should: (a) Keep his weight back, (b) Grab the back of the victim, preferably at the waist, (c) Keep his own body between the victim and the shore, and finally, (d) pull gently.

Use of Floating Objects

When the victim is too far away to be reached with an arm, leg, pole or other object; the rescuer should look for a floating object which can be thrown. Floating objects helpful in rescue are of two types: with or without line attached.

With proper instruction, unattached buoyant objects can be used for rescue. If a kickboard or "flutter" board is available, push it to the drowning victim, give the victim instructions to hold onto the sides and kick to safety. If a lifejacket, vest, or cushion is nearby, throw it to the person in trouble. Give the victim instructions to hold it to his chest and propel himself toward shore by kicking his legs.

Throwing of Objects

Buoyant objects with a line attached are more desirable for use in an elementary form of rescue. An innertube can be attached to a rope and thrown to a victim. Small plastic floats used by children are not suitable because of the possibility of puncture, air loss, or lack of buoyancy.

A plastic gallon container such as that used for milk makes a good homemade buoyant throwing device. Fill the container with an inch or two of water, attach a 15 to 20 foot rope securely to the handle and keep it near the shore or on the pier. Be sure to secure the rope end to one wrist or under one foot before throwing. Use an underhand throw for full extension of the jug and rope. Talk to the victim throughout the rescue process.

A buoyant ring with a rope attached may be available. It may be thrown in the same manner as the water filled gallon jug. At a pool, the buoyant ring is called a "ring buoy". Lifeguards are trained to use it for rescue.

Three important points to remember when throwing any kind of buoyant object with a rope attached are: 1) maintain contact with one end of the rope by stepping on it or tying it to the wrist, 2) if the rope is coiled, place it on one opened hand and let the rope uncoil naturally as the ring or jug is thrown underhand, and 3) always throw the object beyond the victim and slowly pull it into the victim who then grabs on and is pulled to safety.

DROWNPROOFING

The drownproofing technique is a skill used for staying afloat and progressing toward shore in an emergency. When an individual is thrown from a boat into unfamiliar waters or is too tired to swim, drownproofing is a good self-rescue technique.

To learn this skill, stand in chest deep water. Take a deep breath and let the body submerge slightly. Extend the arms forward at shoulder level. At the same time, lean forward and spread the legs as in a giant step. Then press the arms down toward the thighs and squeeze the legs together. Slide the hands up along the sides of the body and then out in front of the body as the knees bend and the legs separate in preparation for the next stroke. This will cause the body to move forward and upward toward the surface where another breath may be taken. Forward progress can be made without a lot of wasted energy. After practicing in chest deep water, practice in deep water.

In an actual emergency, the survival stroke can be very effective, if the shoreline or help is near enough to see. Continue to lean slightly forward and repeat the arm press and leg squeeze motions to make continuous movement forward in the water. Relaxing will keep the body nearer the surface and facilitate faster progress. Use of this technique in very cold water may increase the possibility of hypothermia since the head is immersed in the water.

H.E.L.P. AND HUDDLE POSITIONS

The H.E.L.P. and huddle positions are used to prolong survival in the water. H.E.L.P. stands for *Heat Escape Lessening Position*. (1) An individual who falls into cold water fully clothed and wearing a *Personal Flotation Device* (PFD) should use the H.E.L.P. position to increase his survival time. The clothes should be left on. Draw the knees up with the legs crossed as if in a sitting position. Cross the arms over the chest. Wait for help.

The *Huddle position* is a survival technique used when three or more victims are in cold water with clothing and PFD's on. The idea is for three or four people to place their arms on each others shoulders and huddle together in a small circle. This provides warmth as well as moral support until help arrives. Neither the H.E.L.P. nor the Huddle position should be used in white water or in other river currents.

SEARCH AND RECOVERY PROCEDURES

Speed in finding a person who has slipped below the surface of the water is essential for survival. Establish the exact location of the submerged person. Scuba divers with the proper equipment are preferred to the use of other search and recovery methods. They should be summoned immediately in murky waters or where swift currents are present. Untrained individuals should not attempt to make a swimming rescue. They should seek help as quickly as possible.

Search From a Pier or Pool Deck

If the water is clear and the victim is visible on the bottom, rescue is possible. There are several items that could be used to reach the victim. At pools, there is usually a long pole with a hook on the end. It is commonly called a "Shepherd's Crook". Usually some training is necessary to use it, but in an emergency anyone may use it to lift an unconscious person from the surface of the water or from the bottom of the pool. A boat hook may also be used to catch onto the bathing suit and bring the victim to the surface.

Group Search from Shore

The human chain composed of individuals holding each other's wrists with arms extended can be used effectively when the location of the victim is uncertain. When waters up to chin level have been combed by the human chain with no success, individuals who have been trained in lifesaving techniques should continue the search.

Clarity of the water and a warm water temperature favor a quick rescue. Deep, dark murky waters and a cold water temperature plus high waves or currents make a rescue more difficult.

IMMERSION WHILE CLOTHED

When a boat suddenly tips over, catches fire, or sinks, passengers often find themselves fully clothed in deep water. Individuals caught in this situation should not panic. They should survey the situation and plan a strategy for getting to safety.

If a life preserver is thrown into the water, put it on. If the shore is a short distance away, it may be best to swim to safety. Removal of shoes may make the swim easier. The shoes may be removed, tied together with the strings, and hung around the neck. They can then be put on upon reaching shallow water. This may help to prevent injury caused by walking on sharp rocks.

Disrobing

In water of moderate temperature, removal of shoes and outer clothing may reduce the weight and drag on the body. If a PFD is not available and rescue is not imminent, disrobing is suggested unless the water is very cold.

Remove the shoes first one at a time, then remove the pants, leg by leg and finally remove the shirt or blouse. It is best to use the jellyfish float position for each part of the removal process, coming to the top of the water for air as often as needed.

Inflation Techniques

Inflation techniques are used to create improvised flotation devices out of long pants and long-sleeved shirts which have been removed in the disrobing process. Having removed the shoes and socks, the next step is to remove the pants one leg at a time. Bring the pants to the surface while treading water. Tie the legs of the pants together in a knot, or tie each leg in a knot. Zip or button up the front of the pants. Holding the waistband open at each side, put the pants behind the head. Pull them quickly over the head and down into the water. Gather the waistband while keeping it below the surface of the water. The pant legs should be filled with air forming a buoyant object to rest on. If air does not fill the legs of the pants the first time, try holding the waistband just below the water surface with one hand, and splashing air into the pants by pushing the water down just in front of the open pants. Gather the waistband together or pull the belt through the loops tightening the band to hold air. Another method of inflating the pants is to submerge below the surface of the water, open the waistband which must be under water, and blow air up into the pants. After air has filled the pant legs, return to the surface and draw the band together. The pants are ready to be used for an improvised PFD.

It is possible to inflate a long sleeved shirt that has not been removed. Button up the shirt, blow air in between the second and third buttons. A pocket of air will be formed in the shoulders and upper back of the shirt. The shirt will serve as an effective buoyant device as long as air remains trapped. Tying the bottom of the shirt tightly around the waist will keep the air in the shirt for a longer period of time.

Hypothermia

Hypothermia means lack of (hypo) heat or warmth (thermia) to the body. In common usage, the term has come to mean a serious threat to the body in cold weather, cold water or when the body temperature falls to a dangerous level. This level varies with the age, size, and physical condition of the individual.

In cold water (37 degrees Farenheit), an unclothed person of average build will only survive 20-30 minutes. In water of 47 degrees Farenheit, the same person will collapse and likely drown in 80-90 minutes. Survival time will double, if the individual is fully clothed. High levels of body fat will also increase the individual's ability to survive in cold water. (2)

Breathing difficulty occurs immediately after being thrust into very cold water. Do not attempt to swim unless the shore is near or it is too dangerous to stay in the area. Relax, and float quietly, breathing will return to normal.

Even skilled swimmers will drown if they attempt to swim a long distance in very cold water. In one instance, a boatload of young Marines was overturned in icy waters. All of the men drowned before they could swim the 300 yards to shore.

When floating or waiting for rescue in cold water, movement to stay warm is not recommended. Exercising in very cold water will cause the body to lose heat at an accelerated rate. Therefore, the survival time will actually be shortened.

USE OF LIFEJACKETS AND OTHER PFD'S

A personal flotation device (PFD) which is used in a small craft must be approved by the United States Coast Guard. The Coast Guard approval stamp and the weight bracket for each PFD is clearly indicated on the back of each acceptable PFD. There are five types of approved PFD's. They are commonly called lifejackets, vests, or cushions. PFD's vary by type, size, purpose, amount of buoyancy, and weight classification. By Federal law, PFD's must be stored on all small craft, one for each person aboard. It is preferable that non-swimmers in the craft wear the PFD. Only good swimmers and those who have been trained to don a PFD while in the water should be allowed to go boating **without** wearing one.

Left to right: Type II PFD and Type I PFD

Type I PFD

The Type I PFD is the typical lifejacket with a back and a front. The front fastens together, often with a full belt as well as ties or a zipper. It is an approved device designed to keep a person in a vertical or near vertical position with the face out of the water. The life jacket must have 20 pounds of buoyancy. Due to the high buoyancy level, these jackets are most often used for whitewater rafting and other high risk water sports.

Type II PFD

The Type II PFD or "vest" is the most common, least expensive type. It has a collar, but no back. It ties in the front at neck level. It has a belt which goes around the body and buckles or snaps in the front to secure the two front sections to the chest. With 15.5 pounds of buoyancy, it keeps the body in a face-up vertical position. Vests come in sizes ranging from 20 pounds for a child and over 200 pounds for an adult. The only drawback to the vest is that the collar may become irritating after wearing it for a long period of time.

Type III PFD

The Type III PFD is similar to the Type I PFD in design and to the Type II PFD in buoyancy capacity. It is a small jacket commonly used in water skiing. It allows greater turning ability than the Type I and is less irritating than the Type II PFD. It is approved for use in all sizes of boats. One version of the Type III PFD is a long zippered jacket with a drawstring around the body. This jacket which contains 15.5 pounds of buoyancy may be used in rafting or kayaking.

Type IV and V PFD's

A cushion is an example of a Type IV PFD. Cushions are throwable devices for rescue found in boats more than 16 feet in length. A cushion is a square object with two straps sewn on opposite sides of the square.. These straps which are one and a half times longer than a side, are attached at the corners. They are designed so that the arms can be put through them while in the water. The cushion fits across the individual's back and allows him to easily float on his back. They may be used in place of other types of PFD's in canoes, kayaks, and boats less than 16 feet long.

Type V PFD's are for restricted use only. They are not currently approved for use on recreational boats.

SMALL CRAFT SAFETY

Knowing some important facts about boarding and debarking small craft may prevent capsizing. If care is not taken and the boat overturns, knowing how to survive in a capsized situation can save lives. Small craft applies to all categories of water craft up to 25 feet in length.

Two fundamental principles govern entering or leaving a small boat. The first is to maintain a crouched position when entering to keep the center of gravity of the body low. The second is to make sure that the body weight is evenly distributed from side to side and front (fore) to back (aft) to prevent tipping the boat.

Boarding

When boarding a boat tied to a pier, make sure it is secured at the front (bow) and back (stern). If it is not secured by ropes, have someone hold the top of one side (gunwale) of the boat to the pier for boarding. If entering a canoe or rowboat alone from a pier, bend down and grasp both gunwales (tops of the sides). Place one foot in the center of the bottom of the craft. Keep low as the other foot is brought over the gunwale and placed on the bottom near the center of the craft. In a crouched position, holding onto the gunwales carefully move to the desired position at either the bow or stern of the craft for steering. If care is not taken, unexpected waves from passing boats may prove to be hazardous.

When boarding a canoe from the shoreline, be sure that the majority of the canoe is in the water. If not enough water is under the canoe and a large person or two enters the craft, it will become bound to the bottom and make launching impossible. To board, grasp the gunwales, step in the center of the canoe with one leg, use the other foot to steady the canoe and finally step into the center of the canoe. A lone paddler should keep low, hold on to the gunwales and step forward in front of the mid-ship thwart. The paddler should kneel leaning against the mid-ship thwart for greater control and stability.

Debarking

Basically, to get out or debark from a small craft, the best technique would be to reverse the boarding procedures. In general, hold both gunwales, crouch low, keep the weight centered in the boat or canoe while moving toward the bow which is on shore or anchored to a pier. Then place one foot outside of the boat on firm footing, and transfer the weight to that foot while removing the other foot from the center of the boat and the hands from the gunwales.

Changing Positions

Changing positions should not be necessary during a short trip in a small craft. However, there are people who insist on switching places in midstream. In a canoe, it is much easier and safer to go ashore, exit and re-enter in the new positions. If changing is done, keep in mind three basic principles. First, only one person should move at a time. Second, keep the weight low and centered in the craft at all times. Third, keep the craft trimmed or balanced from side to side and fore to aft at all times. This can be accomplished by leaning to opposite sides.

Capsizing or Swamping

Capsizing means overturning a craft. Swamping means that a boat or canoe is filled with water. Most modern small craft are designed to stay afloat when overturned. When a rowboat or canoe overturns, it usually stays afloat. Hold on to the hull of a rowboat and kick hard toward shore or wait until help arrives. A canoe will stay entirely on top of the water and a pocket of air will be formed underneath it. In the event of a sudden storm, passengers may get under it for protection. If several people are involved, it is best to hold on to the craft and wait for assistance. If people become tired, they may hold each other's wrists across the keel (the bottom) of the overturned craft.

If the craft is upright, but filled with water, it will not sink. It is possible to swim into the boat or canoe and slide or roll to a sitting position on the bottom of the craft. Once it is steady, it can be hand paddled to shore.

NECK AND BACK INJURIES

Lifting a victim who has a serious neck and/or back injury from the water can be dangerous. The procedure should only be done by trained Emergency Medical Technicians or water safety personnel. However, certain principles should be followed to help save the life of a potential paraplegic (two limbs paralyzed) or quadriplegic (four limbs paralyzed).

If the person is found face down, turn him to a face-up position. This can be done by carefully approaching the victim from the side. Reach under the victim with one arm. Line the forearm up with the sternum while firmly supporting the chin with the hand along the jawbone. Cup the other hand at the back of the head and place the arm on the back in line with the spinal column. With locked wrists, squeeze the forearms together. While maintaining this position, roll the victim over by submerging under one side of the victim and returning to the surface on the other side. This should turn him to a face-up position. Retain this grip on the victim until help arrives.

If a spinal break is suspected, do not remove the victim from the water. Wait until a backboard or similar hard flat object the length of the body is available. Float the backboard underneath the person and secure him to it.

If the victim is not breathing, give artificial respiration immediately. Open the airway by using the jaw thrust method. Hold the head in a rigid position so no further damage may occur.

RESCUE BREATHING

Mouth to Mouth

Rescue breathing is a method of artificially reviving a person who has stopped breathing. Many methods have been tried from ancient times to the present. These include: tickling the feet, using hot coals on the feet, hot air bellows, putting a person on the back of a prancing horse, the chest pressure-arm lift method, the back pressure-arm lift method, the Sylvester method, and finally the mouth to mouth or mouth to nose method. This method came to us from one of the oldest books, *The Bible.* In II Kings 4:34, it says that Elisha used a mouth to mouth technique on a boy presumed dead and his skin became warm and he lived.

Establish whether or not the victim is conscious and in need of artificial respiration. To determine this, shake the person gently and ask "Are you alright?" If there is no response, call for help. Make sure that the person is lying in a supine position (on the back). If it is necessary to turn the victim from a prone or front lying position, move the body as one unit since the extent of injury is not known. Place one hand on the forehead and push down gently until the jaw is jutting straight up. It may be necessary to use the thumb and two fingers of the other hand on the bony part of the chin to pull the mouth open. This opens the airway.

Bend down with your ear near the victim's mouth to feel for the warmth of the breath. At the same time look to see if the chest rises, and listen for a sound from the mouth. Pinch the victim's nostrils shut with the thumb of the hand which is resting on the victim's forehead. The rescuer should form a seal by covering the victim's mouth with his mouth. He should blow into the victim's mouth. Repeat with a second breath. Each breath should take about two seconds. Pause three seconds between each breath (for an adult). Watch the victim as the fingers slide from the chin down the neck to the location of the carotid artery on the side of the neck. Check the pulse for at least 5 seconds,but not more than 10 seconds. If there is a pulse, but there does not seem to be any breathing, call out to anyone around who can hear and say "The victim has a pulse, but is not breathing, call 911." Then re-position the head, pinch the nostrils shut, place your mouth on his mouth and breathe in once every five seconds for several minutes. Check the pulse to be sure that the heart is still beating. continue rescue breathing until help arrives or the person starts breathing on his own.

Mouth to Nose

Mouth to nose breathing uses exactly the same procedures as described above except that the rescuer shuts the mouth with one hand and breathes into the nose instead of the mouth. This should only be used when there are extensive cuts to the mouth or when the person has a disease such as Hepatitis.

For a child (age 1-5) use the same procedures except breathe in the mouth or nose once every four seconds and give a smaller breath of air. For a baby (up to one year) give small puffs of air, and breathe in once every three seconds. For babies, it is best for the adult rescuer to place the mouth entirely over the baby's mouth and nose in administering rescue breathing.

Mouth to Stoma

On a rare occasion, a person with a hole in the throat and a tube sticking slightly out of the hole may be encountered. This tube called a stoma, is placed in the throat during a laryngectomy. This surgery is necessary due to throat cancer or emphysema. For rescue breathing in this instance, breathe into the tube the same way as described for administering the mouth to mouth procedure to an adult.

CARDIOPULMONARY RESUSCITATION (CPR)

At times, the victim who is unconscious and not breathing will also be without a pulse. In that case, the rescuer must administer CPR. CPR is a technique for alternating a combination of rescue breathing and chest compressions to restore the victim's heart and lungs. "*Cardio*" means heart, "*pulmonary*" means lungs, and "*resuscitation*" means to revive. Hence, the term "Cardiopulmonary Resuscitation".

CPR is a technique which is beyond the scope of this text. It should be administered by an individual who has received the appropriate training under the auspices of an organization such as the American Red Cross. This is an important skill, well worth the time of 4-8 hours of instruction needed to master it. Every person who spends time in and around the water should become certified in CPR.

SUMMARY

Those who engage in swimming activities will at some time experience muscle cramps, currents or water weeds. In order to prevent panic, which could lead to a full blown emergency, the swimmer needs to know what to do in each of these situations.

Everyone who spends time near the water should be aware of what could be done to assist another individual who gets into a dangerous situation. At the same time the student should be cognizant of his own limitations in helping others. He should know how to reach a victim and pull him to safety without endangering his own life. The student should be alert to items found in the vicinity of the water that may be helpful in making a non-swimming rescue.

Since it is not uncommon for individuals to fall into water while fully clothed, know the procedures for disrobing and using clothing for flotation. Be knowledgeable about hypothermia and its effects on the body in order to make an intelligent decision related to the feasibility of disrobing.

A person who uses small craft should be familiar with proper procedures for boarding the craft, debarking and changing positions in the craft. He should also be prepared for an emergency in case the craft turns over. Associated with small craft is a set of federal rules and regulations related to the use of lifejackets on various types of craft. Small craft users should be knowledgeable about regulations related to using lifejackets on their craft.

First aid procedures such as caring for neck and back injuries, rescue breathing and CPR are important to users of aquatic facilities. Each year hundreds of swimmers dive into shallow water, hit their heads causing back and/or neck injuries. Proper care must be taken to save lives and prevent further injury. In drowning situations, it is necessary to use rescue breathing to revive a victim. CPR may also be needed.

Knowledge and skills related to all of the topics discussed in this chapter will serve to make the swimmer as well as those around him safer in the aquatic environment. Some of the skills discussed need to be practiced periodically in order to maintain proficiency.

REVIEW QUESTIONS

1. Why is it safer to take a canoe to shore before changing positions than it is to change in the middle of the lake or river?

2. List five items that could be used to extend to a swimmer who is in difficulty. (Try to list items that were not discussed in this chapter.)

3. Should an individual who has fallen into very cold water take off a heavy jacket? Explain.

4. How could a non-swimmer or poor swimmer save the life of a friend who was drowning near the pier?

5. How does rescue breathing differ when administered to a small child rather than an adult?

SELECTED REFERENCES

1. American National Red Cross. (1981). *Swimming and Aquatics Safety.* Washington, DC: The American National Red Cross.

2. American National Red Cross. (1974). *Lifesaving, Rescue and Water Safety.* Washington, DC: The American National Red Cross.

3. Lanoue, Fred R., (1950). *"Some Facts on Swimming Cramps".* Research Quarterly 21, 235.

4. Young Men's Christian Association. (1986). *On the Guard, The YMCA Lifeguard Manual.* Champaign, IL: Human Kinetics.

CHAPTER 12
Your Future as a Swimmer

The acquisition of swimming skills and the knowledge of safety precautions around the water will open up a lifetime full of enjoyable water experiences. Whether a novice or expert swimmer, young or old, male or female, housewife or business person; all will have many opportunities for recreational pursuits in the water.

WATER SAFETY COURSES

Some individuals may desire to advance their levels of swimming expertise. Both the American Red Cross and the YMCA offer advanced water safety courses. The Red Cross courses include:

- Advanced Lifesaving — A course designed to teach personal and group rescue and survival skills. The prerequisites include being at least 15 years of age and having the ability to swim continuously for 500 yards.
- Lifeguarding — A course designed to teach personal and group rescue and survival skills. The prerequisites include current Advanced Lifesaving, CPR, and First Aid certificates and the ability to pass several timed swimming tests.
- Water Safety Instructor (WSI) — A course designed to enable an individual to teach all American Red Cross (ARC) swimming courses. The prerequisites include being 17 years of age and holding a current Advanced Lifesaving certificate.

- Water Safety Instructor Trainer (WSIT) — After years of teaching ARC swimming classes, an instructor may request to become a WSIT. If there is a need for an Instructor Trainer, the local ARC chapter recommends the individual for the training and certification process.

- Other certification courses include: Boating, canoeing, kayaking, sailing, basic rescue, and adapted aquatics.

The YMCA offers certification courses as follows.

- Aquatic Leadership — A course which is a prerequisite for all other aquatic leadership training. It includes information on mechanics physiology, safety, and basic lifesaving as well as general knowledge related to the YMCA organizational structure.

- Lifeguarding — A course designed to train a lifeguard for employment at a pool, lake or surf beach.

- Instructor or assistant instructor certification is offered in the following areas of specialization.

competitive swim coach	aquatic
competitive swim official	preschool program
synchronized swimming	springboard diving
aquatics for special populations	aquatic facility manager
camp waterfront director or assistant	progressive swimming
physical fitness through water exercise	arthritis aquatic program

- Instructor training for scuba diving — A series of courses to prepare the instructor to teach basic scuba, advanced scuba, cave, coral reef, ice, search and rescue, scuba lifesaving and accident management.

- Aquatic Director — A course designed to qualify individuals to direct aquatic leadership training programs. Prerequisites include a current YMCA Aquatic Instructor certificate with at least one year of teaching experience, a minimum of three years leadership in YMCA programs and completion of an Aquatic Director Seminar.

PERSONAL PHYSICAL FITNESS

The individual who has developed mobility skills and some of the basic strokes in swimming has all of the necessary qualifications for using swimming as a physical fitness activity. Both competitive and non-competitive programs are available in most communities. Opportunities include water exercise classes, Master's swimming programs and triathlons.

Water Exercise

Water exercise courses are offered by many colleges and universities,YMCA's, YWCA's, and community recreation programs. They go by a variety of names such as, Aquacises, Swimnastics, Aquarobics, and Hydrarobics. Classes are designed to use the water as a medium for exercise. They may include: calisthenic type exercises, running in the water, using jugs for resistance or modifying aerobic dance routines for use in the water. Deep water exercises such as running are included in many classes.

Water exercise classes are beneficial to individuals of all ages. They are particularly beneficial to individuals who have arthritis, since the water supports the body as it moves.

Individuals who have had an injury while participating in other fitness activities frequently use water exercise in order to continue training while recuperating.

Masters Swimming

For competitive swimmers beyond college age, there is a program called *"Masters Swimming."* This program offers swim competition for ages 25-90 for both men and women. For those who swim regularly for fitness, this is an enjoyable recreational activity. Masters Swimming programs are open to anyone including those who have never been on a swim team, but would like to train with a coach and improve their skills. Masters Swimming competition is by age groups in five year increments ranging from the 25-29 age group all the way up to the 90's. With new clubs forming so rapidly, it would be advisable to consult a local chapter of the Amateur Athletic Union (AAU) office which would have current information on Masters swimming organizations.

Triathlon

Triathlon competition is composed of three separate sports: swimming, bicycling, and running. It is the newest of the marathon events and perhaps the fastest growing sport in the world.

One person or a team of two or three people compete by first completing a swim, then without any rest, a bicycle ride, and finally a run. The distance of each of the three parts are pre-determined by a local meet committee. Places are determined by the total time required to complete the three events. An individual competes in all three events or a team of people may each compete in one part of the triathlon. Prizes are awarded accordingly.

The Mini-Triathlon is the term used to designate a shortened version of the triathlon. It attracts a large number of amateur participants. It is not uncommon on a Saturday morning to see 500-700 participants arriving to start a triathlon with a brisk half-mile swim in a lake, coming out of the water with bodies shedding water as they jog along flag lined paths to the bicycle holding area, donning bike shoes and speeding off for a 10-15 mile ride, and returning to start a 5k run (3.2 miles). About 10% of the participants compete in teams of two or three, in which one may swim and run while a second person does the bike event, or any other combination of events. They do it for the sense of achievement, the fitness challenge, and to obtain the T-shirt souvenir.

The most strenuous form of the triathlon is called the "Iron Man" which held annually in Hawaii. Participants must qualify for the Iron Man by finishing in the top three places or meeting a time standard in a qualifying event. It is by far the most physically exhausting for man or woman. Each participant must perform all three events within one day. The swim is performed in the ocean (2.2 miles), the bicycle route encompasses 112 miles, and the run is a full marathon, (26 miles, 385 yards.)

The hardest part of the triathlon is the swim. For many of the athletes, it is the weakest of the three events. Many participants have had little instruction or training in swimming. However, most of the athletes have had considerable experience in cycling and running. Cycling and running are leg-dominated sports but swimming is an arm-dominated sport. When training, the triathlete concentrates on the weakest of the three skills. This has brought a surge of interest in the sport of swimming.

SWIMMING ON THE GO

Business Travel

Busy executives who travel from city to city and hotel to hotel as a part of their job, soon discover that a regular schedule of exercise is difficult to maintain. Most new hotels have built facilities to accommodate the busy traveler. Many have included an indoor or outdoor swimming pool for use by their patrons. This greatly facilitates the traveler's ability to continue with his fitness program. Remember this when making reservations. Discover the difference a good swim makes on the body at the end of a long day. Fifteen to twenty laps will leave a person refreshed, relaxed, feeling fit and ready for a good night's sleep and a brand new day.

Vacation Travel

What vacation is complete without taking a bathing suit along? Whether staying in motels along the route, or at a leisurely vacation spot on a lake or near a beach, a time of enjoyment in the water is pleasurable. Vacation time is a time to learn to swim better, to learn a new water sport, or to teach your children or friends how to swim.

When preparing for a trip, be sure to pack a bathing suit for each member of the family. Some pools require caps for girls and women with long hair. Stick a cap in the suitcase before taking off, just for good measure.

To avoid problems while on vacation, give children full attention around the water. Make sure that they observe common safety rules which include:

✔ Never swim alone.

✔ Do not run on pool decks.

✔ Do not dive into shallow water (five feet deep or less.)

✔ Do not carry glass containers onto the pool deck.

✔ Do not engage in horseplay in or around the pool.

WATER SPORTS

With some swimming skills and a comfortable feeling both in water and below the surface, water sports could open up a new vista of recreational and fitness activities. Adult men and women may discover water polo at the local "Y", or at a new fitness center. Scuba diving lessons are available from dive shops, local colleges or universities, YMCA's or adult education evening classes. Sailboating and sailboarding are increasing in popularity at local lakes in the summer. Classes in the techniques of handling all small craft are usually available in lake areas at the beginning of each summer season. Canoe trips down rivers and lakes can be taken by all. Some choose a calm trip down a lazy river and others select a white-water river trip with swirling waters and rough currents. For most trips all equipment and a guide can be obtained at boat liveries. Many state parks also offer canoes for rent.

Kayaking is an Olympic sport, but it is not yet popular as a water sport in this country. However, interest in the sport is growing. Kayaks may be rented at certain boat liveries or purchased at local boating outfitters. Instruction in kayaking may be obtained by contacting the American Red Cross chapter in your area.

Water skiing can be learned with some instruction and a good boat driver. After learning to get up out of the water on two skis, the skier will soon discover how to slalom (ski on one ski). One of the latest ideas in skiing is the "jet ski", a mini boat that one stands on to steer and literally skis alone through the water.

Snorkeling is a water sport that one would engage in most often around coral reefs. It is really for underwater sight seeing, while swimming near the top of the water with mask, fins, and snorkel gear on.

Other water sports for recreation and enjoyment include white-water rafting and inner tubing. Some water sports do not require advanced swimming skills, but they do require a good healthy respect for large bodies of water and a knowledge of safety techniques in times of emergency.

SYNCHRONIZED SWIMMING

Clubs and classes in synchronized swimming, also known as "water ballet", are burgeoning since the sport became popularized during the 1984 Olympics. Adaptations and variations of strokes are used to create beautiful ballet motions. A great deal of strength, breath control, and body control is needed to perform the motions with beauty and ease. Local "Y's" may have classes where the skills can be learned. On the West coast and in Florida, clubs have been organized to encourage synchronized swimming.

TEACHING YOUR CHILDREN

Parents who have only limited knowledge of swimming skills themselves may not be able to teach their own children. But there are many things that they can do to ready a child for good experiences in the water. The first step is to go with the child to the pool or beach. Let the child enjoy the shallow water by splashing and playing in it. Hold him by the hands and let him go beneath the surface of the water briefly. When the child emerges, smile broadly and grasp the child to your chest for comfort and assurance of safety. Becoming comfortable in water settings, both above and below the surface of the water is necessary before formal teaching can begin.

Seek out other families with children of similar ages and arrange water activities together. Some suggestions might include planning a summertime pool party with simple water games in the shallow end, or taking the kids to a big Water Slide for the day. Some states have water parks with almost all water activities. Inner tubing is a good family activity.

Precautions must be taken with very young children. They must be carefully and continually watched while they are in or near the water. Do not leave them unattended, not even to answer the telephone. Consider putting flotation devices on small children so that they can not slip unnoticed beneath the surface of the water. Watch siblings who may innocently take little ones into deep waters. Know rescue breathing in case the child accidentally falls below the surface for a minute or two.

Once a child has become familiar with the water and enjoys being in it, consider putting him in a swimming class or providing private lessons. Check the qualifications of instructors and make sure that the student-teacher ratio is small. Some children may need to repeat a swimming class several times before they pass it. Children should continue taking lessons until they become competent swimmers. (ARC Intermediate or Swimmer Level.)

OPPORTUNITIES FOR THE DISABLED

The aquatic opportunities are increasing for the disabled as they are in all other sports. Scuba diving is popular with the orthopedically impaired. Paraplegics and triplegics with the proper gear are very successful. A new book titled *Scuba Diving with Disabilities* by Robinson and Fox is excellent for training in the sport.

Sailing, wind surfing, skiing, white water rafting and kayaking are aquatic sports suited for the hearing impaired. The visually impaired particularly love sports where the smell of the water, sound of the waves, and the feel of an object beneath them accompanies the activity. Such sports would include canoeing, sailing, aquarobics, and inner tubing.

Students with cerebral palsy may enter into any aquatic activity in which they feel comfortable and safe. A Danmar sectional raft gives full support in the water. A PFD with head support, the Delta float system, an inflatable collar, or a ski belt may be used to assist for support until independence is achieved. All types of boating would be most enjoyable. Scuba diving would also be appropriate.

With advanced technology providing the disabled with myriads of new devices for assistance in sports, the horizon is endless. In the near future, it would be within the realm of reason to see a cerebral palsied student water skiing or sailboating with the proper bracing and safety devices.

SUMMARY

The individual who has learned the basics of swimming has opened the door to a multitude of new activities. He can start with advanced courses offered by the American Red Cross or the YMCA in order to improve his skills in one of many aquatic activities. As he gains skill and confidence in his abilities, he may even elect to become an instructor of various aquatic activities.

Those who are looking for an alternative to jogging, may find that water exercise or lap swimming fills their needs. These same programs can be used by those who are recuperating from an injury induced by another sport. Those who prefer to be involved in a competitive program may find the Masters Swimming Program tailored to their needs. While individuals who like a variety of high level fitness activities may enjoy the triathlon.

Today swimming is an activity that can be enjoyed year round, at home or away. The business man can take advantage of hotels and motels that provide swimming facilities. In this way he can continue his physical fitness routine wherever he goes. Families can also experience increased enjoyment as they take time to swim at the beach or at the hotel/motel pool while on vacation.

Once an individual becomes a water sports enthusiast, he will continually find new ways to be challenged. A listing of water sports and activities would include Scuba diving, water skiing, canoeing, kayaking, boating, surfboarding, sailing, fishing, and snorkeling. Each of these activities will lead to many hours of enjoyment on the water.

Parents need to introduce their children to aquatic activities at an early age. They should teach them to have a healthy respect for the water, but avoid instilling a morbid fear. Parents should encourage their children as they learn the basics of swimming and water safety.

REVIEW QUESTIONS

1. What has caused the increase in the popularity of synchronized swimming as a sport in the United States?

2. Where can an individual go to get the necessary training in Scuba diving?

3. What is the most important thing that parents can do to encourage their children to participate in swimming activities?

4. What can an athlete do to improve the swimming phase of his triathlon?

5. What opportunities are available at your college or university for swimming as a physical fitness activity?

SUGGESTED READINGS

1. Kochen, C. L. & McCabe, J., (1986). *The Baby Swim Book*. Champaign, IL: Leisure Press.

2. Maglischo, E. W. & Brennan, C. F., (1985). *Swim for the Health of It*. Palo Alto, CA: Mayfield.

3. Shea, E. J., (1986). *Swimming for Seniors*. Champaign IL: Leisure Press.

APPENDIX A
FITNESS SWIMMING

Swimming has become a very popular mode of training for the fitness enthusiast. Each day thousands of people across the country take to the water as part of their fitness routine. Others join them occasionally as a change of pace activity or for the purpose of continuing an exercise program by using a non-weight bearing activity while recuperating from an injury.

The student who would like to begin a swimming fitness program or the one who wants to incorporate swimming into this regular workout schedule should be cognizant of basic information related to physical fitness. Information regarding frequency, duration, intensity and swimming target heart rate, warm-up and cool down has been included in this section.

FREQUENCY

Frequency refers to how often an individual should exercise in order to experience the benefits of a cardiovascular exercise program. Most research indicates that excellent results can be obtained by working out four or five times per week. Time spent in additional training sessions will not necessarily result in increased benefits.

DURATION

Duration refers to the total time used for a training session. When beginning an exercise program, each workout should last 15 to 20 minutes. After a few weeks of training, workouts should be extended to a minimum of 30 minutes. Individuals who exercise 30 to 60 minutes during each workout will experience changes in physical fitness level.

INTENSITY AND SWIMMING TRAINING
HEART RATE

The term, intensity, refers to how much effort is exerted during the workout. A swimmer who works out 30 to 60 minutes four to five times a week will not experience a cardiovascular training effect unless he works at an intensity which is great enough to overload (tax) the cardiovascular system.

In order to determine the intensity of the workout, the swimmer should monitor his heart rate by taking his pulse at the carotid artery at various times during the workout. The swimming target heart rate should be somewhat lower than the target heart rate of land activities. This may be due to one or more factors:

1. The heart rate pumps more efficiently when the body is in a prone position.
2. The breathing pattern is changed while in the water.
3. Immersion in cool water may lower the resting heart rate. (2)

Table one shows the swimming target heart rate for swimmers between the ages of 18 and 50.

Table 1

SWIMMING TARGET HEART RATE ZONES FOR SWIMMERS BETWEEN THE AGES OF 18 and 50

AGE	THR ZONE	AGE	THR ZONE
17	135 - 168	34	125 - 153
18	135 - 167	35	124 - 153
19	134 - 167	36	124 - 152
20	134 - 166	37	123 - 151
21	133 - 165	38	123 - 150
22	132 - 164	39	122 - 149
23	132 - 163	40	121 - 148
24	131 - 162	41	121 - 147
25	130 - 161	42	120 - 147
26	130 - 160	43	120 - 146
27	129 - 159	44	119 - 145
28	129 - 159	45	118 - 144
29	128 - 158	46	118 - 143
30	127 - 157	47	117 - 142
31	127 - 156	48	117 - 142
32	126 - 155	49	116 - 141
33	126 - 154	50	115 - 140

WARM-UP

The swimmer should warm-up prior to the workout. The warm-up will gradually increase muscle temperature. This will help to prevent soreness and help to avoid injuries. A good warm-up should include stretching as well as swimming 100 to 300 yards at a slow, easy pace. During this phase of the total workout, the swimmer is also able to mentally prepare for the main part of the workout. Examples of stretching exercises can be found in references listed at the end of this appendix.

COOL-DOWN

The last portion of the workout is the cool-down. During this time, the swimmer continues swimming, but at a slower pace. This will allow muscular contractions to assist the venous system in returning blood to the heart from the extremities. The cool-down may include stretching exercises as well as swimming. The cool-down period should last about five minutes.

THE WORKOUT

There are a number of training methods which are used by fitness swimmers and competitive swimmers. The fitness swimmer who uses a variety of these training methods will find it easier to maintain a high level of motivation. Training mehtods include:

1. **Distance Swimming.** This is the technique most frequently used by fitness swimmers. It involves continuous swimming of 400 yards or more. This type of swimming is used to increase endurance. However, the swimmer must be aware of the tendency for the intensity level to fall off, if he does not continually check the pace clock during his swim.

2. **Fartlek Training.** As used in swimming, fartlek training is a system that alternates fast and slow swimming. In this type of training, the swimmer may swim a fast 100 yards followed by a slow 100 yards.

3. **Interval Training.** Interval training uses a series of repeat swims alternated with periods of rest. If the workout calls for 10 x 50 on 1:15, the interval includes the time to swim the 50 yard distance and rest before repeating the distance. Interval training is an excellent technique for developing both speed and endurance.

4. **Repeat Training.** This type of training is used occasionally by competitive swimmers. It calls for a near maximum effort followed by a long rest prior to repeating the distance. It helps to increase speed and anaerobic capacity.

Workout Terminology

1. **Pull** — Use a pull-buoy or PT tube to support the legs while practicing the arm motion of the stroke.
2. **Kick** — Use a kickboard while practicing the leg motion of the stroke.
3. **Broken Distance** — Distance swims which are broken into smaller segments with very short rest periods (5 to 10 seconds) between segments.
4. **Swim** — Use both the arm and leg motions for the stroke. Unless otherwise noted, use the front crawl.
5. **Individual Medley (IM)** — A swim in which the four competitive strokes are used in the following order: Butterfly, Back Crawl, Breaststroke, and Front Crawl.
6. **Pace Clock** — A large clock placed on the wall or on the deck at the end of the pool which is used by the swimmer to check his swimming pace and times for intervals.

WORKOUT OPTIONS
WARM-UP

Level I

1. Swim 4 x 25 easy
2. Swim 2 x 50 easy
3. Swim 100 easy
4. Swim 25
   Pull 25
   Kick 25
   Swim 25

Level II

1. Swim 100 easy
2. Swim 200 easy
3. Swim 100
   Pull 50
   Kick 50
4. Kick 2 x 100
5. Swim 100, Pull 100

Level III

1. Swim 200 easy
2. Swim 300 easy
3. Swim 200
   Kick 100
4. Swim 300 easy, change
   strokes on each 100
5. Swim 100
   Pull 100
   Kick 100
6. Pull 150
   Kick 150

MAIN WORKOUT

Level 1

1. 10 x 25 on 50
2. Swim 25, 50, 75, 100, 75, 50, 25. Rest after each distance.
3. Broken 300. Rest 10 seconds after each 25.
4. 4 x 50 on 1:45
5. 2 x 200 on 5:30
6. Swim 400
7. 4 x 100 on 3:15
8. 8 x 75 on 2:45
9. 300, 200, 100. Rest 30 seconds between.

Level II

1. 10 x 50 on 1:30
2. Swim 50, 100, 150, 200, 150, 100, 50. Rest 30 seconds between.
3. Broken 500. Rest 10 seconds after each 100.
4. 10 x 75 on 2:30
5. 4 x 200 on 4:30
6. 4 x 100 IM on 2:45
7. Swim 1000
8. 8 x 150 on 3:30
9. 20 x 25 on 45 seconds

Level III

1. 2 x 10 x 50 on 1:00. Rest 1:30 after first set.
2. 10 x 100 on 2:15
3. 3 x 400 on 6:30
4. Broken 800. Rest 10 seconds after each 100.
5. Swim 100, 200, 300, 200, 100. Rest 30 seconds between.
6. 900 fartlek — alternate hard and easy 50's
7. 4 x 200 IM. Rest 30 seconds between.
8. 8 x 125 on 2:45
9. Swim 1500
10. 20 x 25 30.

COOL-DOWN

Level I

1. Swim easy 100 any stroke
2. Kick easy 50
   Pull easy 50
   Swim easy 50

Level II

1. Swim 200 easy,
   any stroke
2. Kick easy 100
   Pull easy 100

Level III

1. Swim easy 300, any stroke
2. Swim easy 200
3. Kick 100

DIRECTIONS FOR USING WORKOUT OPTIONS

1. Determine your level as follows:

   Level I — Workout distances up to 1000 yards.
   Level II — Workout distances ranging from 1000 to 2000 yards.
   Level III — Workout distances over 2000 yards

2. Select an option from the list of warm-up activities.
3. Select an option from the list of cool-down activities.
4. Select items from the main workout section.
5. As your fitness level improves, make adjustments in the workout as follows:
   a. Increase the total distance.
   b. Move to the next level.
   c. Decrease the time for the interval.

SELECTED REFERENCES

1. Brems, M. (1979). *Swim for Fitness.* San Francisco: Chronicle Books.
2. *Executive Fitness.* Volume 17, number 4, page 4.
3. Katz, J. (1981). *Swimming for Total Fitness: A Progressive Aerobic Program.* Garden City, NY: Dolphin Books/Doubleday.
4. Maglischo, E. W. (1982). *Swimming Faster.* Palo Alto, CA: Mayfield.
5. Maglischo, E. W. & Brennan, C. F. (1985). *Swim for the Health of It.* Palo Alto, CA: Mayfield.

APPENDIX B

SOURCES OF EQUIPMENT AND SUPPLIES FOR THE AQUATICS PROGRAM AND THE AQUATICS ENTHUSIAST

The following list of suppliers from around the country carry a large assortment of accessories for the swimmer as well as equipment used in the aquatic program. Each of the suppliers list their products in a catalog that can be obtained by writing to them. Many of the companies listed have a toll free telephone number.

Adolph Kiefer & Associates

1750 Harding Rd, Northfield, IL 60093 1-800-323-4071
Supplier of suits, kickkboards, pullbuoys, PT tubes, goggles, masks, fins, snorkels and other items.

Aquatic Enterprises, Inc.

1189 Westmoreland Dr., Harrisonburg, VA 22801 (703) 433-1109
Supplier of goggles, PT tubes, hand paddles, kickboards, caps and other items.

Aquatic World

28 Kenton Lands Rd., PO Box 18580, Erlanger, KY 41018 1-800-354-9789
Supplier of suits, sweats, goggles, caps, chamois and other personal items.

Halogen

4653 West Lawrence, Chicago, IL 60630 1-800-824-9682
Supplier of pool and safety equipment.

William B. Hugg, Inc., Swimming Accessories

1721 Kirks Lane, Dresher, PA 19025 1-800-255-7946
Supplier of suits, caps, goggles, chamois, earplugs, nose clips, hand paddles, kickboards, pullbuoys, and other items.

Metro Swim Shop

1221 Valley Road, Stirling, NJ 07980
Supplier of Speedo suits, and personal equipment

The Finals

21 Minisink Ave., Port Jervis, NY 12771
Supplier of suits and accessories.

Recreonics

7696 Zionsville Rd., Indianapolis, IN 46268 1-800-428-3254
Supplier of suits, goggles, pullbuoys, kickboards, chair-lifts and other equipment for the swimmer and the pool.

The Swim Shop

742 Fesslers Lane, PO Box 100110, Nashville, TN 37210 1-800-251-1412
Supplier of suits, sweats, chamois, kickboards, goggles, pullbuoys and other equipment and supplies for the swimmer.

T.J.'s Swim and Trophy

236 S. Salem St., PO Box 1450, Dover, NJ 07801
Supplier of Hind suits and sweats, and personal equipment as well as pool supplies.

Walters' Swim Supplies, Inc.

11712 N. River Rd., Mequon, WI 53092 1-800-558-0428
Supplier of Speedo, Hind and Arena suits and sweats as well as kickboards, goggles, hand paddles, masks, pullbuoys, swimming technique charts, caps, snorkels, The Sammy and other items of equipment for the swimmer and the pool.

World Wide Aquatics

509 Wyoming Ave., Cincinnati, Ohio 45215 1-800-543-4459
Supplier of suits, sweats, caps, bags, goggles, towels, and other accessories.

APPENDIX C

TIPS ON OVERCOMING FEAR
OF THE WATER

Fear occurs when an individual anticipates a situation in which he may be frightened. The individual experiences feelings of anxiety about what may happen. This anxiety is so strong that it prevents the individual from participating in the dreaded activity. The fear may or may not be related to a previous unpleasant experience.

Many people of all ages experience a fear of water. This fear prevents them from enjoying a multitude of aquatic activities. In the case of adults, fear affects not only the life of the individual, but the lives of other family members. The fearful adult may even pass his fear on to his children.

It is possible to overcome even a deep seated, long term fear of the water. However, this will only occur when an individual has reached a state of readiness in relation to learning to swim. To be successful the individual must have an overpowering desire to overcome his fear of water and learn to swim.

Readiness must be maintained, especially during the early stages of learning. To maintain the state of readiness, the student must experience success and encouragement. Students and teachers must work together in an effort to create an atmosphere in which the determined student can experience success on a daily basis.

Students who are committed to breaking the grip of fear of water on their lives should study and follow the tips listed below.

- Enroll in a water exercise class which uses the shallow end of the pool to do a variety of activities other than swimming. Participating in such a class prior to enrolling in a formal swimming class may serve to build confidence and reduce anxiety.

- Try to spend time relaxing prior to going to a swimming class. Think about the pleasures related to the water, the reasons for wanting to learn to swim and the successes that have been experienced (even the smallest ones). Picture yourself swimming with ease and enjoying the water.

- There will be other adults in the class who have fears. Share your fears with them.

- Work together in class with one or two partners. Develop a trust and confidence in each other. Encourage each other.

- Establish realistic short term and long term goals.

- Don't try to rush or become discouraged, if progress is slow. Each step, no matter how small, will bring you closer to your goal. Many years of fear will not be overcomed overnight.

- Discuss your fears with the instructor. In most cases he has worked with many students who have had fears and he will be able to give you the support you need.

- Do not try to skip steps in the learning process. Master each skill before going to the next.

- Adult beginners frequently have the greatest success when they begin with skills which allow them to keep their faces out of the water.

- Go to open or recreational swim sessions to practice the skills that you are learning. The more you practice, the more confidence you will have in your own abilities and the faster you will make progress.

- Never say never. Keep an open mind. Be willing to try new things. You are capable of doing anything that you really want to.

- Knowledge and your ability to reason are assets in overcoming fear. Find out what skills you will be learning during the next class period and read the text before attending class. Be prepared to ask questions about skills when you do not understand.

- Sometimes your instructor will use games to help you learn a skill. The game may be a simple one that you learned in grade school. Don't let that bother you. Play it enthusiastically, it will help take your mind off your fear as you practice a skill or get used to the water.

- Most adults just want to learn a stroke well enough to participate in recreational activities. Find the one stroke that you can perform best and become good at it. Then go on to another.

- Trust your instructor. He will not ask you to do anything that you are not capable of.

It is never too late to learn to swim or to overcome a fear of the water. Just because you missed the opportunity to learn to swim when you were a child, doesn't mean that you can't learn. As long as you keep trying and keep motivated you will succeed.

APPENDIX D

ASSESSMENT OF SWIMMING STROKES

The following grading procedure may be used to assign points for each stroke based on the number of essential items that are performed. This information may be put in chart form with the names of the strokes and essential items at the top and the students names on the side, or vice versa.

Grading System: Assign points from 1 to 5 based upon skill performance.

5 — Excellent — Stroke form and coordination
4 — Very Good — Slight correction needed
3 — Good — Two stroke elements missing
2 — Poor — Three stroke elements missing
1 — Very Poor — Most elements missing.

BASIC STROKES

Elementary Backstroke

— Body position, water at ear level, hips, heels high.
— Thumbs lead up body, elbows point downward.
— Legs whip kick as arms pull, should finish together.
— Knees not above the water at any time.
— Arms against body, legs together, toes pointed at end of glide.

Sidestroke

— Head on side in water to corner of mouth.
— Bottom arm (extended) bends as it pulls.
— Top arm comes up and pushes close to body.
— Scissor kick (top leg forward) begins at same time as the top arm pushes.
— Top arm stops on inner thigh.
— Legs end together, no crossover or drift allowed.

Front Crawl

— Head held at hairline level when pointing forward.
— Kick 10" deep, kick up toward surface, 6" spray.
— Raise elbow and wrist above and on recovery.
— Open eyes, relax hand and wrist.
— Use "S" arm pull pattern, elbow high.
— Exhale in air pocket, chin down.
— Breathe each stroke, on same side.
— Shoulder rotation 45 degrees on breathing side and 25 degrees on non-breathing side.
— Arms should move continuously and exit water at hips.
— Inhalation complete by time elbow passes shoulder.

Breaststroke

— Body prone, hips flat and near surface.
— Head starts out with mouth at water level.
— Arms pull, elbows high, until hands are beneath the shoulders, then elbows collapse.
— Head lowers to hairline as arms extend and legs whip around and down.
— Knees part to about shoulder width and stay inside the feet during the whip kick.
— Feet are flexed and push with soles of the feet.
— Watch for distinct sections of the pull, kick, and glide in that order for good rhythmic control.
— Lift head to breathe again as hands begin to pull.

Back Crawl

— Stretch body out in back glide position.
— Use crawl kick, spray about 6" high.
— Hand enter water just outside shoulder line, little finger leading.
— Shoulder drops, elbow bends and hand pushes toward bottom, no windmill action allowed.
— Turn palm of hand down at end of push.
— Watch for continuous action of arms and legs.

ADVANCED STROKES

Overarm Sidestroke

— Body position and kick same as sidestroke.
— Top arm uses overarm recovery as in crawl, enters water near chin, presses back to inner thigh.
— Coordination of arms and legs are the same as the sidestroke.

Trudgen Crawl Stroke

— Head at hair line level as in front crawl.
— Arm motions are the same as the front crawl.
— Three flutter kicks alternate with a single scissors kick.
— Scissors kick is performed while exhaling into the air pocket.

Inverted Breaststroke

— Body stretched out as in back glide position.
— Arms begin overhead and together.
— Arms sweep to sides and press through to the thighs.
— Arms come up body with thumbs leading and then slip under the head.
— Just before arms extend, legs execute the whip kick.
— Watch for knees out of the water and other faulty elements of the whip kick as mentioned above under the elementary backstroke.
— Execute a glide before starting arm press again.

Butterfly Stroke

— Body prone and straight, arms begin to lift.
— Use a bent arm, drive out and in for first part of force phase.
— Keep elbows up until press toward feet is complete.
— Press feet downward and use knees to whip lower legs to full extension.
— Upbeat of kick must have straight leg position for major part of the recovery phase.
— Raise head only to lower lip, jut chin out to catch a breath.
— Bring arms all the way to hips before exiting water.
— Kick downward faster than upward on dolphin kicks.

APPENDIX E

DIRECTORY OF AQUATIC ORGANIZATIONS AND ORGANIZATIONS THAT INCLUDE OR PROMOTE AQUATIC ACTIVITIES IN THEIR PROGRAMS

Amateur Athletic Union (AAU)
AAU House, 3400 W 86th St., Indianapolis, IN 46268 317) 872-2900

American Alliance for Health, Physical Education, Recreation and Dance (AAHPERD)
1900 Association Drive, Reston, VA 22091
(703) 476-3400

American Athletic Association of the Deaf
3916 Lantern Drive, Silver Spring, MD 20902

American National Red Cross
17 th & "D" St. N.W., Washington, DC 20006

American National Standards Institute (ANSI)
1430 Broadway, New York, NY 10018

American Public Health Association
1015 15th St. N.W., Washington, DC 20005

Aquatic Exercise Association
PO Box 497, Port Washington, WI 53074 (414) 375-2503

Athletic Institute
200 Castlewood Dr., North Palm Beach, Florida 33316

Council for National Cooperation in Aquatics
901 W New York St., Indianapolis, In 46223 (317) 638-4238

FINA
1750 E. Boulder St., Colorado Springs, CO 80909

International Swimming Hall of Fame
1 Hall of Fame Dr., Fort Lauderdale, Florida 33316

National Collegiate Athletic Association (NCAA)
PO Box 1906, Shawnee Mission, KS 66201

National Recreation and Parks Association (NRPA)
3101 Park Center Dr., Alexandria, VA 22302

National Safety Council
444 N. Michigan Ave., Chicago, IL 60611

National Spa and Pool Institute
2111 Eisenhower Ave., Alexandria, VA 22314 (703) 833-0083

National Swimming Pool Foundation
10803 Gulfdale, Suite 300, San Antonio, TX 78216 (512) 525-1227

National Wheelchair Athletic Association
2107 Templeton Gap Rd, Suite C, Colorado Springs, CO 80907 (303) 597-8330

Recreation Safety Institute
100 Arrival Ave., Ronkonkoma, NY 11779

Senior Games Development Council
200 Castlewood Dr., North Palm Beach, FL 33408 (305) 842-3600

Special Olympics Inc.
1350 New York Ave., N.W., Suite 500, Washington, DC 20005 (202) 544-7770

United States Diving
901 W New York St., Indianapolis, IN 46223

United States Swimming
1750 E. Boulder St., Colorado Springs, CO 80909

United States Synchronized Swimming
901 W. New York St., Indianapolis, IN 46223

United States Water Polo
1750 E. Boulder St., Colorado Springs, CO 80909

US Association for Blind Athletes
55 W. California Ave., Beach Haven Park, N.J. 08008

YMCA of the USA
101 N Wacker Ave., Chicago, IL 60606 (312) 269-0520

APPENDIX F

PERIODICALS OF INTEREST TO THE AQUATICS ENTHUSIAST

Aquatics
PO Box 1147, Skokie, IL 60076-9736

Canoeing and Kayaking
PO Box 3146, Kirkland, WA 98083

Cruising World (Boats)
Cruising World Publications, Inc., 5 John Clarke Road, Newport, RI 02840

Dive Magazine
PO Box 45497, Los Angeles, CA 90045

Recreonics (Pool Equipment)
Recreonics Corp., 7696 Zionsville Rd., Indianapolis, IN 46268

SCUBAPRO Diving and Snorkeling
PO Box 14003, Orange, CA 92613

Skin Diver
6725 Sunset Blvd, PO Box 3295, Los Angeles, CA 90078

Swim Magazine
PO Box 45497, Los Angeles, CA 90045

Swimming Technique
PO Box 45497, Los Angeles, CA 90045

Swimming World & Junior Swimmer
PO Box 45497, Los Angeles, CA 90045

The Swimming Times
Sport Shelf, Box 634, New Rochelle, NY

Triathlete Magazine
1127 Hamilton St., Allentown, PA 18101

APPENDIX G
AQUATIC WORD PUZZLE

Fifty words related to aquatics and the materials covered in this text have been hidden in the puzzle below. Words may be in a horizontal, vertical, or diagonal direction. They may be printed either forward or backward. Circle each word as you find it and list it on the following page. A complete list of words can be found on page 172.

```
G X S E K O R T S T S A E R B D E T R E V N I Y
O N A B U C S G D D M E R E M G M G G E R E M E
G WI Q U U B E O R Q J A C V T B B I F U N Z K
G O Z L D H F K L T A C T E T S A D V L E D O O
L B O L L X B O P D H G U F E C V E F O R M Y R
E U Z U T U S R H H F L V K K V A H O A Q U T T
S S L T P M C T I M U T O C I C S E O T E T R S
X WY Y D T E S N R A R R O S D N B K V K N U K
G M A O M S V E P A T A R E P O K T I C S E D C
F N F L U O N D G S W S R A R C N D R D A M G A
T S R C F B A I T L S WC P I E E A G W M O E B
WC E F P L L S F A WN H K G C M O E L X M N Y
E L Q F L R A L T I I O G I A P H T N S I G H R
E P U H R E I I U A M N T F P A P F D A S D S A
D M E F R L U M O P G I R R O K X X I F C E E T
S T N B Y S U R S D X U G U E O I O V E A O V N
R L C L M R S T G N S L E Y B D Y C E T N B A E
N O Y I C T A T R I A T H L O N N E K Y O A WM
O R Q L F C Y T I S N E T N I D U U K S A M C E
S S U I C R A W L L E K R O N S R S P I K E S L
E F K T R E S I S T A N C E D R A U G E F I L E
MI WS H C A O R P P A A E B U T T E R F L Y S
```

Aquatic Word Puzzle

List words as you find them.

1. _____	26. _____
2. _____	27. _____
3. _____	28. _____
4. _____	29. _____
5. _____	30. _____
6. _____	31. _____
7. _____	32. _____
8. _____	33. _____
9. _____	34. _____
10. _____	35. _____
11. _____	36. _____
12. _____	37. _____
13. _____	38. _____
14. _____	39. _____
15. _____	40. _____
16. _____	41. _____
17. _____	42. _____
18. _____	43. _____
19. _____	44. _____
20. _____	45. _____
21. _____	46. _____
22. _____	47. _____
23. _____	48. _____
24. _____	49. _____
25. _____	50. _____

Answers to Aquatic Word Puzzle

Approach
Back Crawl
Beach
Breaststroke
Buoyant
Butterfly
Canoe
Cap
CPR
Cramp
Crawl
Dive
Dolphin
Drag
Elementary Backstroke
Frequency
Fulcrum
Glide
Goggles
Intensity
Inverted Breaststroke
Kickboard
Lifeguard
Mask

Momentum
Olympics
Pike
Pool
Prone·
Pull Buoy
Rescue
Resistance
Safety
Scuba
Sculling
Sidestroke
Snorkel
Sunburn
Surface Dive
Swim
Swimsuit
Triathlon
Trudgen
Turn
Undertow
Waves
Weeds
Whip Kick

APPENDIX H
REVIEW TEST

Note: This test can be used by the student as a review, or selected questions may be used by the instructor for the final exam.

TRUE-FALSE

Circle the correct response; "T" for true statements, "F" for false or partially false statements.

T F   1. Swimming is the best fitness activity for all ages.

T F   2. Annually, less than 5,000 drownings occur in one year.

T F   3. The Iron Man Triathlon requires a marathon run.

T F   4. Swimming is excellent for handicapped individuals.

T F   5. Vigorous swimming can raise the pulse rate which leads to a training effect.

T F   6. The first personal flotation device was a "mussek".

T F   7. Swimming was an event in the ancient Olympic games.

T F   8. "Asceticism" means elevation of the body over the mind.

T F   9. Competitive swimming originated in Japan.

T F   10. The American Indians invented the stroke now known as the crawl.

T F   11. The butterfly stroke was the last competitive stroke invented for competition.

T F   12. The first summer games for the deaf included swimming.

T F   13. Nylon women's swimsuits are best for lap swims.

T F   14. Earplugs can be molded to fit an individual's ears, preventing water from entering.

T F   15. Goggles help protect eyes from heavily chlorinated water.

T F   16. Hand paddles are most frequently used for strengthening and correcting arm strokes.

T F   17. Snorkels with large tubes and purge values at the base are best.

T F   18. Chair lifts enable disabled students to enter the pool easily.

T F 19. The "Sammy" is used as a towel.

T F 20. A certain amount of fear of the water is both normal and healthy.

T F 21. Swimming at an unsupervised beach is acceptable at times.

T F 22. When caught in a river current, the swimmer should swim diagonally toward shore.

T F 23. PFD's are required on sailboats.

T F 24. Air mattresses are good flotation devices for children.

T F 25. The sting of a jellyfish can cause death.

T F 26. Poison ivy rashes can be spread in water.

T F 27. An individual with an ear infection should stay out of the water.

T F 28. Firm massage will relieve muscle cramps.

T F 29. Athlete's foot requires constant care and treatment.

T F 30. Swimming in pools in winter increases the incidence of colds.

T F 31. Swimming may be beneficial to throat infections.

T F 32. Women can swim safely during menstrual periods.

T F 33. Swimming in cold water elevates the pulse rate.

T F 34. Buoyancy helps the disabled to move better in water than on land.

T F 35. The back float position is basic to learning the inverted breaststroke.

T F 36. The prone kick glide includes the flutter kick.

T F 37. Bobbing is a skill which should be learned prior to learning rhythmic breathing.

T F 38. Form drag is created by body movement through the water.

T F 39. Newton's first law is the Law of Acceleration.

T F 40. The elementary backstroke uses a whip kick.

T F 41. The scissors kick is used exclusively with variations of the sidestroke.

T F 42. The front crawl is the fastest and most efficient stroke known to man.

T F   43.   In the back crawl, the arms are in continuous motion.

T F   44.   The arm pull of the back crawl can be described as a question mark.

T F   45.   The breaststroke is a resting stroke.

T F   46.   Hearing impaired students can learn to swim well.

T F   47.   Dropping the hips down helps when "turning over" from the prone to the supine position.

T F   48.   Changing directions is like making a "U" turn.

T F   49.   The flutter kick is used only in underwater swimming.

T F   50.   Hyperventilation is an important technique which is used to improve underwater swimming ability.

T F   51.   Surface dives can be used for rescues.

T F   52.   The overarm sidestroke was a competitive stroke at one time.

T F   53.   Open turns can be learned easily by the visually impaired.

T F   54.   Closed turns are used mainly by competitive swimmers.

T F   55.   The single trudgen stroke uses one scissors kick.

T F   56.   The trudgen crawl uses two different kicks.

T F   57.   The inverted breaststroke uses an arm pull which starts above the head.

T F   58.   The dolphin kick was adopted for use in the butterfly after 1950.

T F   59.   Never dive into water that is less than seven feet deep.

T F   60.   "Feet first, first time" is a good rule for diving into unfamiliar waters.

T F   61.   The body rotates faster in a dive if the body is tucked.

T F   62.   The sitting dive is an easy technique for beginners.

T F   63.   The standing dive with spring should be done only on the diving board.

T F   64.   Moving the fulcrum back increases the amount of spring that can be obtained from the diving board.

T F   65.   A three step approach and a hurdle are commonly used for most springboard front dives.

T F 66. Sudden twisting when caught in underwater weeds can cause further entanglement.

T F 67. Reaching assists are first options for rescues close to pool decks or piers.

T F 68. Buoyant objects can be thrown to tired or struggling swimmers.

T F 69. Drownproofing is a method of moving in the water while staying afloat.

T F 70. The "huddle" is a survival technique used to maintain body heat.

T F 71. The shepherd's crook can be used at a pool for rescuing an unconscious victim on top or under the water.

T F 72. Disrobing may be necessary if rescue is not imminent.

T F 73. Clothing may be inflated for keeping afloat.

T F 74. Hypothermia may claim the life of an excellent swimmer in very cold water.

T F 75. The Type I PFD is a vest.

T F 76. The Type II PFD is a cushion.

T F 77. In boarding a boat, keep your weight low.

T F 78. Changing positions in a canoe is best accomplished on shore.

T F 79. Canoes float when overturned.

T F 80. Rescue breathing was mentioned in the Old Testament of the Bible.

T F 81. Give two quick breaths to begin rescue breathing.

T F 82. Mouth-to-stoma rescue breathing is used for those who breathe through the throat.

T F 83. CPR involves resuscitation of the heart and lungs.

T F 84. The American Red Cross offers a course in canoeing and kayaking.

T F 85. Masters swimming is designed for competitive swimmers over 50 years of age.

T F 86. Water exercises are very beneficial to individuals with arthritis.

T F 87. Triathlons are only for the most expert swimmers.

T F 88. The "Iron Man" is traditionally performed in Hawaii.

T F 89. Fitness swimming in hotel pools is possible in every large city.

T F 90. Water ballet classes are popular on the West Coast.

T F 91. A WSI certificate is required to teach American Red Cross swimming courses.

T F 92. Lifeguarding is a new American Red Cross course which includes CPR and First Aid certification.

T F 93. The YMCA offers a training course for Aquatic Directors.

T F 94. Sailboarding is increasing in popularity on many lakes.

T F 95. Snorkeling is used mostly for underwater sight seeing.

T F 96. Paraplegics and triplegics can experience success in scuba diving.

T F 97. Danmar rafts support cerebral palsied students in water.

T F 98. Parents should teach children how to love being in the water before teaching them how to swim.

T F 99. This book was written by two college swimming instructors.

T F 100. There are over 20 water sports and activities available which are attractive for the person who has learned the basic skills of swimming.

BIBLIOGRAPHY

Aaron, J. E., Bridges, A. F., Ritzel, D. O., (1972). *First Aid and and Emergency Care.* New York: Macmillan.

American National Red Cross. (1977). *Adapted Aquatics.* Washington, DC: American National Red Cross.

American National Red Cross. (1981). *Canoeing and Kayaking.* Washington, DC: American National Red Cross.

American National Red Cross. (1974). *Lifesaving, Rescue and Water Safety.* Washington, DC: American National Red Cross.

American National Red Cross. (1974). *Lifesaving and Water Safety Courses*: *Instructor's Manual.* Washington, DC: American National Red Cross.

American National Red Cross. (1974). *Manual for the Basic Swimming Instructor.* Washington, DC: American National Red Cross.

American National Red Cross. (1981). *Standard First Aid and Personal Safety.* Washington, DC: American National Red Cross.

American National Red Cross. (1981). *Swimming and Aquatics Safety.* Washington, DC: American National Red Cross.

American National Red Cross. (1969). *Teaching Johnny to Swim.* New York: Doubleday.

Anderson, B. (Ed.). (1975). *Sportsource.* Mountain View, CA: World Publications.

Arlott, J. (Ed.). (1975). *The Oxford Companions to World Sports and Games.* London: Oxford University Press.

Bland, H. (1979). *Competitive Swimming.* England: E. P. Publishing Ltd.

Brems, M. (1979). *Swim for Fitness.* San Francisco: Chronicle Books.

Brown, T. & Hunter, R. (1978). *Concise Book of Snorkeling.* Agincourt, Canada: Gage.

Collis, M. & Kirchoff, B. (1974). *Swimming.* Boston: Allyn and Bacon.

Counsilman, J. E. (1968). *The Science of Swimming.* Englewood Cliffs, NJ: Prentice-Hall.

Dept. of Health and Human Services. (1983). *Aqua Dynamics,* Washington, DC: The President's Council on Physical Fitness and Sports.

Eaves, G. (1969). *Diving.* New York: A. S. Barnes.

Fairbanks, A. R. (1963). *Teaching Springboard Diving.* Englewood Cliffs, NJ: Prentice-Hall.

Gaughran, J. A. (1972). *Advanced Swimming.* Dubuque, IA: Wm. C. Brown.

Getchell, B. (1983). *Physical Fitness: A Way of Life.* New York: John Wiley & Sons.

Getchell, B. (1987). *The Fitness Book.* Indianapolis, IN: Benchmark.

Harris, M. M. (1969). *Basic Swimming Analyzed.* Boston, MA: Allyn and Bacon.

Hickok, R. (Ed.). (1977). *New Encyclopedia of Sports.* New York: McGraw-Hill.

Hovis, F. (Ed.). (1976). *The Sports Encyclopedia.* New York: Praeger Publications.

Huey, L. & Knudson, R. R. (1986). *The Waterpower Workout*. NY: New American Library.

Jarvis, M. A. (1972). *Enjoy Swimming*. London: Faber and Faber, Ltd.

Jones, J. A. (1988). *Teaching Guide to Cerebral Palsy Sports*. (3rd ed.). Champaign, IL: Human Kinetics.

Knopf, K.; Fleck, L. & Martin, M. M. (1988). *Water Workouts*. Winston-Salem, NC: Hunter Textbooks.

Krasevec, J. A. & Grimes, D. C. (1985). *HydroRobics* (2nd ed.). Champaign, IL: Leisure Press.

Kochen, C. L. & McCabe, J. (1986). *The Baby Swim Book*. Champaign, IL: Leisure Press.

Lanoue, F. G. (1950). *Some Facts on Swimming Cramps*. Research Quarterly. 21, 153-155.

Mackenzie, M. M. & Spears, B. (1982). *Beginning Swimming*. Belmont, CA: Wadsworth.

Maglischo, E. W. (1982). *Swimming Faster*. Palo Alto, CA: Mayfield.

Maglischo, E. W. & Brennan, C. F. (1985). *Swim For The Health of It*. Palo Alto, CA: Mayfield.

Menke, F. G. & Palmer, P. (Eds.). (1978). *The Encyclopedia of Sports*. (6th ed.). Southbrunswick, NY: A. S. Barnes.

Michaud, E. & Anastas. L. L. (1988). *Listen to Your Body*. Emmaus, PA: Rodale Press.

Midtlyng, J. (1982). *Swimming*. (2nd ed.). Philadelphia, PA: Saunders College Publications.

Miller, D. I. (1984). *Biomechanical Characteristics of the Final Approach, Step, Hurdle and Takeoff of Elite American Springboard Divers*. Journal of Human Movement Studies, 10, 189-212.

Miller, D. I. & Munro, C. F. (1984). *Body Contributions to Height Achieved During the Flight of a Springboard Dive*. Medicine and Science in Sports and Exercise, 16 (3), 234-242.

Miller, D. I. & Munro, C. F. (1985a). *Greg Louganis' springboard takeoff: I. Temporal and Joint Position Analysis*. International Journal of Sport Biomechanics, 1, 209-220.

Miller, D. I. & Munro, C. F. (1985a). *Greg Louganis' springboard takeoff: II. Linear and Angular Momentum Considerations*. International Journal of Sport Biomechanics, 1, 288-307.

Morris, D. (1969). *Swimming*. London: Heinemann Educational Books.

Murray, J. L. (1980). *Infaquatics, Teaching Kids to Swim*. West Point, NY: Leisure Press.

National Safety Council, (1988). *Accident Facts*, 1987. Chicago, IL: National Safety Council.

O'Brien, R. F. (1968). *Springboard Diving*. Columbus, OH: Charles E. Merrill.

Oppenheim, F. (1970). *The History of Swimming*. North Hollywood, CA: Swimming World.

Price, F. (1965). *Water Ballet Pageants.* Minneapolis, MN: Burgess.

Prins, J. (1982). *The Illustrated Swimmer.* Honolulu, Hawaii: Honolulu He'e.

Robinson, J. & Fox, A. D. (1987). *Scuba Diving with Disabilities.* Champaign, IL: Human Kinetics.

Russell, A. (Ed.). (1987). *1988 Guinness Book of World Records.* New York: Sterling.

Sanders, R. H. & Wilson, B. D. (1988). *Factors Contributing to Maximum Height of Dives After Takeoff From the 3M Springboard.* International Journal of Sport Biomechanics, 4 (3), 231-259.

Shea, E. J. (1986). *Swimming for Seniors.* Champaign, IL: Leisure Press.

Sherrill, C. (Ed.). (1986). *Sport and Disabled Athletes*: The 1984 Olympic Scientific Congress Proceedings. (Vol. 9). Champaign, IL: Human Kinetics.

Spears, B. (1966). *Fundamentals of Synchronized Swimming.* Minneapolis, MN: Burgess.

Spears, B. & Swanson, R. A. (1983). *History of Sport and Physical Activity in the United States.* Dubuque, IA: Wm. C. Brown, Torney, J. A. & Clayton, R. D. (1970). Aquatic instruction, Minneapolis, MN: Burgess.

Vickers, B. J. (1965). *Teaching Synchronized Swimming.* Englewood Cliffs, NJ: Prentice-Hall.

Vickers, B. J. & Vincent, W. J. (1984). *Swimming.* (4th ed.). Dubuque, IA: Wm. C. Brown.

Whiting, H. T. A. (1970). *Teaching the Persistent Non-Swimmer.* London: G. Bell and Sons.

Young Men's Christian Assn. (1986). *YMCA Progressive Swimming "Splash".* Champaign, IL: Human Kinetics.

Young Men's Christian Assn. (1986). *YMCA Progressive Swimming Instructor's Guide.* Champaign, IL: Human Kinetics.

Young Men's Christian Assn. (1986). *YMCA "On the Guard".* Champaign, IL: Human Kinetics.

Young Men's Christian Assn. (1986). *YMCA Lifeguard Manual.* Champaign, IL: Human Kinetics.

GLOSSARY

Aquatics — sports practiced on or in the water.

Athlete's Foot — a ringworm of the feet, caused by a fungus that thrives on moist surfaces.

Back Crawl — a stroke performed while on the back which uses an alternate over-the-water arm recovery and a flutter kick. It is frequently referred to as the back stroke in competitive swimming.

Back Float — a position on the back in which the swimmer remains as motionless as possible with the back arched and arms and legs extended.

Bobbing — moving the head and body vertically above and below the water; a preliminary skill to rhythmic breathing.

Breaststroke — a stroke performed while in a prone position which uses a simultaneous pull of both arms followed by an under-the-water arm recovery and a leg kick in which the knees bend as the heels are drawn toward the buttocks in preparation for a backward thrust against the water; used as a competitive stroke as well as a resting stroke by recreational swimmers.

Buoyancy — the tendency of a body to be pushed upward by the force of the water in which it is floating.

Butterfly — a competitive swimming stroke performed while in a prone position which uses a simultaneous arm pull followed by a double over-the-water arm recovery and a simultaneous up and down movement of the legs known as the dolphin kick.

Dive — a technique used to enter the water or submerge below the surface of the water. Usually it refers to entering the water or submerging head first.

Dolphin Kick — an undulating movement of both legs together, used in the butterfly stroke.

Drag — a force which acts in opposition to the forward movement of the body through the water.

Elementary Backstroke — a resting swimming stroke performed while on the back using a simultaneous under-the-water recovery of both arms followed by a simultaneous thrust of both arms and a leg kick in which the knees are bent as the heels are drawn toward the buttocks in preparation for a backward thrust against the water followed by a glide.

Extension — a movement of a body part which results in an increase in the angle formed by the adjoining bones.

Fins — rubber or silicone web shaped extensions that are attached to the feet by a strap or slipper which are used in scuba diving and snorkeling.

Flutter Kick — an alternating up and down kicking movement of the legs and feet used in the front and back crawl strokes.

Force Phase — the part of each stroke when the arms and/or legs exert pressure against the water to accelerate body movement.

Front Crawl — a swimming stroke performed while in a prone position in which the arms alternately pull as they move backward through the water and then recover over the surface of the water and a leg kick in which the legs alternately move up and down in the water, also called the freestyle.

Fulcrum — a horizontal bar on which the diving board rests which is used as a point of rotation for the board.

Glide — the part of each stroke at the completion of the force phase where body momentum continues without arm or leg movement.

Goggles — a piece of eye protection used by competitive swimmers to see better underwater and to protect the eyes from excessive burning from pool chemicals; thick plastic lens encased in supple rubber forming a seal around the eyes and attached by a strap behind the head.

Hyperventilation — a series of rapid and deep breaths used by some swimmers in an effort to reduce the amount of carbon dioxide in the lungs prior to underwater swimming; the technique is used in an effort to increase the amount of time a swimmer can remain underwater; dangerous practice that may result in death.

Inverted Breaststroke — a swimming stroke performed while on the back which uses a simultaneous underwater arm pull followed by a simultaneous underwater arm recovery and a whip kick followed by a glide through the water.

Jellyfish Float — a position in the water with knees bent, arms grasped around the knees, head dropped down in the water causing the back to rise and appear at the surface.

Kickboard — a two inch thick hard styrofoam board (1' x 2') with one rounded end, used to support the body while practicing kicks.

Kick Glide — a technique in which the swimmer pushes off into a glide position and begins to kick.

Layout Position — a position used in diving in which the body remains straight with no bend in the hips or the knees throughout the dive.

Level-Off — a technique used to come to a floating position near the surface after jumping or falling into the water.

Mask — an airtight piece of equipment used to cover the eyes and nose for underwater swimming.

Masters Swimming Program — a competitive swimming program for those of post college age composed of regular practice and competitive meets.

Overarm Sidestroke —a swimming stroke performed in a side lying position in which one arm recovers over the water and then pushes back against the water while the other arm pushes water toward the feet and then recovers under the water; legs use a scissors kick followed by a glide to complete the stroke.

PFD — a personal flotation device used by an individual to remain afloat in the water; provides buoyancy to keep the head above water.

Pike Position — a body position in which the hips are flexed while the knees remain straight; used in surface diving and the "jack-knife" board dive.

Prone Float — a position in which the individual is face down with arms and legs fully extended, the back is slightly arched so that the body stays at or near the surface of the water.

Pull — a forceful arm movement used to propel the body in a direction opposite to the force.

Pullbuoy — a piece of equipment composed of two hard styrofoam cylinders (8" - 10" long) attached by nylon rope. It is held between the thighs to support the legs while practicing various arm movements.

Recovery Phase — the part of a stroke where arms and/or legs are relaxed and returning to the starting position.

Rescue Breathing — artificial respiration.

Resistance — a force created by the water which tends to retard movement of the body through the water.

Resting Stroke — a swimming stroke in which a glide is an integral part of its rhythmic pattern, allowing short periods of movement through the water without a simultaneous effort being made; sidestroke, overarm sidestroke, elementary backstroke, inverted breaststroke, and the breaststroke.

Rhythmic Breathing — the alternate breathing in air above water and blowing it out into the water while swimming prone strokes.

Scissors Kick — both knees bend and draw up toward the buttocks where the legs separate in a forward-backward direction and then the extended legs are forcefully squeezed together ending on top of each other; used in the sidestroke, the overarm sidestroke and the trudgen.

Scuba Diving — Scuba is an acronym for "self contained underwater breathing apparatus", which refers to a sport in which the swimmer uses breathing apparatus, mask and fins to explore underwater for extended periods of time.

Sculling — a "figure 8" movement of the hands used to move the body or to help support the body as in treading water.

Sidestroke — a swimming stroke performed in a side lying position in which both arms and legs remain below the surface of the water during both the force and recovery phases of the stroke. One arm pulls while the other arm and legs recover to a position ready for a thrust of the bottom arm backwards and the legs in a scissors action, then concludes with a glide.

Snorkel — a hollow "J" shaped tube used for breathing while swimming at or near the surface of the water with the face in the water.

Surface Dive — a quick movement of the body straight downward in the water, initiated from the surface of the water.

Treading Water — a skill used to keep the head above water in a vertical and stationary position.

Triathlon — a competitive athletic event composed of a swimming race, a bicycle race, and a foot race; performed individually or by teams.

Trudgen Stroke — a swimming stroke performed in a prone position in which the arms move as in the front crawl and the legs move either as in the sidestroke or as in a combination of the sidestroke and the front crawl.

Tuck Position — a body position in which the hips and knees are flexed and the knees are drawn toward the chest; this compact body position is used to increase the speed of the spinning body in somersault dives; it is also used in surface diving.

Turn — a maneuver used to move the body quickly in the reverse direction after reaching the end of the pool.

Whip Kick — a kick where the heels come to the buttocks, knees held about ten inches apart, the feet turn outward and the lower legs whip around and back for the breaststroke (or up, as in the elementary backstroke and inverted breaststroke) thrusting the body forward; legs and knees are together at the end of the kick.

INDEX